Thomas Arnold

PRINCIPLES OF CHURCH REFORM

Thomas Arnold

PRINCIPLES OF CHURCH REFORM

With an Introductory Essay by

M. J. Jackson and J. Rogan

LONDON
S·P·C·K
1962

This edition first published in 1962
by S.P.C.K.
Holy Trinity Church
Marylebone Road
London N.W.1

Printed in Great Britain by
Billing and Sons, Ltd., Guildford and London

CONTENTS

Introductory Essay

by

M. J. JACKSON and J. ROGAN

CONTENTS

EDITORS' NOTE

In preparing this edition and introductory essay we are indebted to the Right Reverend E. R. Wickham, Bishop of Middleton, and to the Reverend A. R. Vidler, Litt.D., Dean of King's College, Cambridge, for many useful criticisms and suggestions.

I

INTRODUCTION

The views of Thomas Arnold were ill-received during his lifetime and after his death. More attention is given to his educational work at Rugby than to his theological ideas, although his detractors do not spare his reputation as headmaster. "He lived in a world of his own, as despotic at his writing desk as in his school, and wielding his pen as if it were a ferule", wrote T. Mozley.[1] The whole range of his theological ideas is rarely seen. The more usual treatment is for his sharp criticisms of the Oxford Movement to be isolated and condemned and the rest ignored. "As a headmaster, his reputation grew steadily, as a social thinker he was soon forgotten completely, while as a religious personality he is still remembered vaguely as an antagonist of Newman", is the summary of a recent biographer of Arnold, T. W. Bamford.[2]

We consider, however, that his theological ideas are important not only for the student of ecclesiastical history but for those who are concerned with the social and theological situation which the Church faces in the contemporary world. When J. B. Mozley wrote in his *Essays Historical and Theological*,[3] "his church reform pamphlet was a leap into a sphere for which he was unfit; and it let out a secret which

[1] *Reminiscences, chiefly of Oriel College and the Oxford Movement.* Vol. 2, Longmans, 1882, p. 52.

[2] *Thomas Arnold,* Cresset Press, 1960, p. 174. Mr Bamford redresses the balance by pointing out that "religious and social affairs occupied the centre of Arnold's thoughts", p. 191.

[3] Op. cit., Vol. 2, 1878, p. 24.

the world might not have discovered else; viz. that he was not a great man", he was less than just to Arnold. Certainly Arnold was a stern critic of the Oxford Movement in its early stages but he died before its full course had run. Yet the very triumph of the Oxford Movement made the use of another perspective difficult and thus affected the nineteenth-century churchman's view of Arnold. Nevertheless Arnold had influence in the Church through such men as Stanley and more largely in the community through responsible laymen. "Few Anglicans have made such an impact upon the secular order or have done it more good. . . . He elevated the political and administrative functions into Christian vocations at every level of the State, just at the time when the nation was becoming the centre of a vast Empire."[4] J. Middleton Murry wrote that Arnold's policy in education was "the inculcation of social responsibility as the direct consequence of Christian belief".[5]

This new Liberalism, of which Arnold was one of the creators, was "much bolder and more independent than the older forms, less inclined to put up with the traditional, more searching and inquisitive in its methods . . . much larger in its views and sympathies . . . it was penetrated by a sense of the reality and seriousness of religion. It saw greater hopes in the present and the future than the Tractarians".[6] The descent of this Liberal attitude may be traced in the nineteenth century through such a person as Mr Gladstone who in early life was specially fond of reading Arnold's sermons aloud and who "in old age said that the Doctor was a 'high, large impressive figure—perhaps more important by his character and personality than his actual work' ".[7] Or again, William Temple as a young man held

[4] *The National Church and the Social Order,* Church Information Office, 1956, p. 87.

[5] *The Price of Leadership,* S.C.M. Press, 1939, p. 60.

[6] R. W. Church, *The Oxford Movement,* Macmillan, 1890, p. 338.

[7] J. Morley, *Life of Gladstone,* Lloyd, 1908, Vol. 1, p. 75; Vol. 2, p. 541.

"the strong conviction that Thomas Arnold was the greatest Englishman of the nineteenth century",[8] and from his teaching Temple had drawn a conception of the Church and State which was for many years to dominate his thought. Alongside his theological ideas we must set his social insights. He was not a social scientist in the twentieth-century sense, but he made telling judgements which revealed how well he understood the social and industrial revolution taking place in his generation. It was not only his theological ideas but also his social perception that led him to radical, unorthodox yet penetrating judgements. "When he died, many, even his opponents, saw him as a keen observer of society with no one else having quite his breadth of vision."[9] *Principles of Church Reform* sprang from a mind at once daring and well informed.

Nevertheless, although "disciples went forth from the school of Arnold determined to bring the consecration of religion into every act of their daily lives",[10] the ideas of Arnold have suffered general neglect. How has this come about? First, the enormous impression which he made upon the English public school system naturally tended to diminish interest in the less successful and spectacular aspects of his life. Secondly, the vigorous cut and thrust of the debates around the Oxford Movement damaged the reputations of most participants. Dean Church considered that Arnold's article in the *Edinburgh Review* was the beginning of a suspicion of the Movement which ran powerfully throughout the nineteenth century, while the impression that Arnold was unorthodox could only be fostered by Wilfrid Ward's alignment of him with Herbert Spencer's

[8] F. A. Iremonger, *William Temple,* Oxford University Press, 1948, p. 93.

[9] T. W. Bamford, ibid., p. 212. Lionel Trilling writes of Thomas Arnold as "touched with the sociological spirit of his century", *Matthew Arnold,* Allen and Unwin, 1939, p. 48.

[10] H. Wakeman, *The Church of England,* Rivington, 1899, p. 464-5.

agnosticism.[11] Thirdly, there are hints spasmodically that the intensity of his character did not make for easy relations at all times. "He seems to have been a learned, pious, virtuous person, without five grains of common sense", said Sydney Smith.[12] This may well have affected his prospects because Melbourne, the Liberal Prime Minister, preferred peace and quiet to new ideas, and the humourless, busy, progressive Arnold represented much which he disliked.[13]

However, men have triumphed over such handicaps before, and the chief reason for Arnold's neglect may well be that the second half of the nineteenth century had different concerns from the first half. Some of the practical reforms which he had urged were passed in the early days of the Ecclesiastical Commission, when Blomfield and his colleagues tackled structural and administrative problems of the Church. A few measures of practical reform satisfied the faint-hearted and those who wanted little change and stilled the cry of the opponents of the Church; while the success of reform tended to divert attention from the basic principles underlying reform with which Arnold was chiefly concerned. Relations with the Dissenters deteriorated over church rates and education so that the ideal of comprehen-

[11] *W. G. Ward and the Oxford Movement,* Macmillan, 1899, p. 58.

[12] H. Pearson, *The Smith of Smiths,* Penguin, p. 263.

[13] David Cecil, *Lord M.,* Constable, 1954, p. 246.

In Greville's *Journals* there is this interesting passage:

> Melbourne told me the other night at Seftons that he had been down to Oatlands to consult F . . . and H . . . about Dr Arnold of Rugby and to ascertain if he could properly make him a Bishop; but they did not encourage him which I was surprised at, recollecting the religious correspondence which formerly passed between them and him. Arnold, however, shocks the High Churchmen, and is not considered orthodox; and Melbourne said it would make a great uproar to put him on the Bench, and was out of the question. He had been reading his sermons, which he thought very able.

Vol. III, p. 325, 18 December 1835.

sion was quite out of the question. Within the Church of England the issues of Ecclesiastical and Biblical authority, the nature of Catholicity and the Ritualist controversies absorbed the energies and thought of the clergy and laity.

Recent years have witnessed a revival in our appreciation of nineteenth-century churchmen and theologians. The readjustment of ecclesiastical perspectives, the new ecumenical situation and our understanding of the need for mission in an industrial society have all combined to revive an interest in Arnold's thought as a missionary theologian and social commentator of insight. We may not agree with his ideas in their entirety: few do with those of any man. However, Arnold and, in particular, his *Principles of Church Reform,* is worthy of consideration to-day.

appointed the bishops of the Established Church, who, not unnaturally, reflected the party's general outlook and opinions.

An incumbent was often drawn from the rural gentry, who themselves were the social backbone of the Tory Party. The assistant curates, drawn largely from another social group, were of no account. The clergy of Jane Austen's novels reflect the general picture. The Church was thoroughly integrated into the existing social order.

The clergy were unconscious of themselves as a separate order. "Enthusiasm" was eschewed; at their best the clergy showed an unostentatious manliness. Of this old High Church school Dean Church wrote: "There was nothing effeminate about it, as there was nothing fanatical; there was nothing extreme or foolish about it; it was a manly school, distrustful of high-wrought feelings and professions, cultivating self-command and shy of display and setting up as its mark, in contrast to what seemed to it sentimental weakness, a reasonable and serious idea of duty."[3] At its worst it became worldliness: "High and Dry", high in its doctrine of the Church, but dry because its theology lacked any dynamic amidst profound social and intellectual changes. It was this aspect which Arnold criticized so severely in his article on the "Oxford Malignants" in the *Edinburgh Review,* believing that such persons attached themselves to Christianity merely because it happened to be established by law. Thus in the midst of great changes the majority of the clergy held to the Tory Party and to the privilege of the National Church, hoping for the best until the tyranny should be past. Part of their difficulty was the lack of effective leadership. Yet when aroused by the Oxford Men in 1833, they displayed a strength surprising even to themselves.

Both the Church and society during the early nineteenth century had been affected by the small but influential

[3] R. W. Church, *The Oxford Movement,* 1891, p. 8.

Evangelical Party. The impetus had come from the Arminianism of Wesley and the Calvinism of Whitefield, whose followers like Hervey, Romaine, Cecil, Venn, Fletcher, and Newton provided the fount of inspiration. Their presence was felt most of all in the agitation for the abolition of the slave trade and to a lesser extent in the promotion of better conditions both in factories and prisons. Unfortunately they never developed a theology which could win over the intellectual mind of England, though their ethos was predominant at court, in the universities, and in the general religion of the land. The Evangelical spirit was expressed in philanthropic work which flowered in noble endeavours and voluntary societies. After the frivolity of the Regency period they encouraged a greater seriousness: duelling died out, sobriety was appreciated, family prayers became more common, and Sabbatarianism revived. Amongst the clergy there was a greater decorum and a higher view of their vocation. Both hunting and drinking declined amongst the cloth.[4] The Evangelicals were, in a phrase, "the moral cement of English Society", and "in the last resort it is to their influence that we must attribute the success of the moral reform which Thomas Arnold and others were effecting at this time in the Anglican public schools".[5] Even though this is true Arnold could never identify himself with them, because he rejected their narrow outlook which caused them to work only in such fields as their straitened consciences would allow. He thought they left great tracts of the national life open to the rule of either natural laws or the devil. The effective penetration needed to build a Christian society could not be inspired by them.

[4] Sydney Smith had a characteristic comment: "If anything ever endangers the Church, it will be the strong propensity to shooting for which the clergy are remarkable. Ten thousand good shots dispersed over the country do more harm to the cause of religion than the arguments of Voltaire and Rousseau." Hesketh Pearson, *The Smith of Smiths,* London, Hamish Hamilton, 1934, p. 146.

[5] E. Halévy, op. cit., Benn, 2nd ed. revised, 1949, Vol. 2, p. 162.

The Church stood in need of reform and indeed under the actual threat of it. The repeal of the Test and Corporation Acts and the passage of the Roman Catholic Emancipation Bill meant a major shift in the traditional Church–State relationship, as Dr Brose has ably pointed out.[6] The result was more than the mere redistribution of church property, it was the termination of the privileged position which penal legislation had given the Church. The Plurality Bills of 1831 and 1832 were "very moderate and liberal" according to the Prime Minister but they were so modified in debate that the result was to show how little the Church could be trusted to reform itself. Public opinion became more and more impatient of abuses which were being so delicately pruned and circumscribed. At this juncture the *Extraordinary Black Book* appeared, whose anonymous author was John Wade, a credulous, prejudiced, but not dishonest man.[7]

The Bishops, it was calculated, controlled but 1,500 out of 11,700 benefices, whose patronage for the most part, therefore, lay with the laity. They regarded a benefice as an item of property and sometimes auctioned benefices to the highest bidder. About 4,000 freeholds, however, were worth not more than £50 a year so that pluralities were sanctioned in order to raise a satisfactory income. The result was that 6,000 benefices possessed non-resident incumbents. In these cases the pastoral work was done by a curate who might be paid less than a day labourer. For example, the benefice of Wetheral and Warwick was worth £1,000 a year, but the curate received £50. Sometimes they received less than £20. Upon these inequalities of income the reform movement fastened, and in particular those between the incomes of bishops and curates.

[6] O. J. Brose, *Church and Parliament, the reshaping of the Church of England, 1828-1860,* Oxford University Press, 1959.

[7] See W. L. Mathieson, *English Church Reform 1815-1840,* Longmans, 1923.

R. M. Beverley's *Letter to the Archbishop of York* was supplementary ammunition to the cause of reform. He assailed the manner of disposing of ecclesiastical offices by borough owners. He attacked the "agreeable obsequiousness" of the bishops and their nepotism. Freedom, he argued, lay in separation from the State, and while few clerics agreed with that, many staunch churchmen, of all shades of opinion, had no high opinion of the average bishop. "The critical condition of the Church", writes W. L. Mathieson, "was sorrowfully admitted by its friends and proclaimed with indecent exaltation by its foes. . . . Had the clergy been alive to their own interest they would long ago have insisted upon an official enquiry."[8]

For the moment the ideas of others were in wide circulation, in particular, those of the Whigs who were in office at this time. Their attitude towards the Church of England was well put by Charles James Fox. "He should be ever a decided friend to our established religion but it should be ever founded on the opinions of the majority of the people." The truth of religion was a fit subject for discussion in parliament. Parliament merely sanctioned that which was most universally approved and allowed it the emoluments of State. Established religion owed its privilege to the elected representatives of the majority of the people. The Whig idea was that of a sect raised to the eminence of an establishment by the favour (and self-interest) of the State.

To many churchmen this was a poor view, but worse followed. The easy-going religion professed by such Whigs as Melbourne appeared scandalous and occasionally blasphemous. Bishop Lloyd wrote to Peel in 1828 summing up Goderich's ministry thus: "Lord Holland, his wife an atheist and himself not far from it. Lord Lansdowne, a confessed Unitarian, Brougham a deist and others whom I

[8] Op. cit., p. 63.

could easily enumerate of the same principles."[9] The need for churchmen to come forward with a positive line of their own was clearly shown when they realized, with pained surprise, that in this conflict the Dissenters would go with the "Godless" and not with "Morality". The Dissenters' objection to the privileges of Establishment was stronger than their horror of the shortcomings of the Whig leaders. Hence Arnold's emphasis on the need to conciliate Dissenters. Because of the Dissenters' strength and attitude he had reservations about the effectiveness of any proposed reforms for the Church of England alone. He believed that no reform of the Church's machinery would satisfy them, but would merely "confirm their separate existence by relieving them from all which they now complain of as a burden. And continuing distinct from the Church, will they not labour to effect its overthrow, till they bring us quite to the American platform?"[10] For this reason it was a basic principle of his to incorporate the Dissenters first into a comprehensive National Church and then to reform its administration. In the prevailing atmosphere of the nation he felt that he could not press for Church Extension by means of government grants. "I cannot press for Church Extension, in the common sense of the term, as a national measure, because I think the mass of Dissent renders it, if objected to by the Dissenters, actually unjust."[11] He felt the same difficulty about Church rates.[12] It is a measure of Arnold's compassion and stature that he could sympathize with the predicament of the Dissenters.

The position formulated by the churchman required

[9] "The Whigs and the Church Establishment in the Age of Grey and Holland" (*History*, June 1960).

[10] A. P. Stanley, *The Life of Thomas Arnold*, John Murray, 1901, Teachers' edition, p. 308. References to Stanley are all to this edition, which has a preface by Sir Joshua Fitch. The American platform meant a state neutral in its constitution towards religion but containing a number of voluntary religious societies.

[11] Op. cit., p. 557.

[12] Ibid., p. 433.

the State to recognize the Church as in some manner different from the sects, or else the Church would have to think of itself as a body distinct from the State, requiring a greater measure of freedom from legislative control. The Church of England needed some sign from the State which recognized it as the National Church. Bishop Blomfield, together with Peel, the agent of the Church's defence and reform, suggested that it needed aid to become the efficient instructress of the people. He chose to defend the Church on the ground on which the Whigs and middle class made their attack: "Utility." When another Whig opinion was that the State founded and supported the Establishment it was inevitable that the debate should take place upon the Church's property and functions. Said the Utilarians: "The Church is not using its endowments for the spiritual and mental culture of the people, therefore these resources should be directed to their proper use." Foremost in this programme of service to culture was the moulding of the character of the people. It was the great passion of the age. Arnold stood for it with great vigour on the Christian side, and accepted the notion that the property of the Church was held in trust (under the control of King and Parliament). Here was another reason why the Church should be comprehensive.

There were signs from different quarters of a desire to cut through the ambiguities of the National Church in a pluralist society—from Philosophic Radicals and Tractarian Dons at Oxford. But the bishops who led the Church in the actual battles were empiricists acting within the context of each situation, accepting the ambiguity of the National Church in a pluralist society and trying to live with it. Blomfield and Peel accepted the reform of Church property for the benefit of religion. They did not admit any change from its original use. The Church had an inalienable right to its own property. Blomfield appealed to the State to help the Church adapt itself to the new situation and was confident that so long as the Church stood as the instructress of the people it would not be disestablished. Co-operation with reform and readiness to serve the people required that the Church should win the people before any great crisis arrived.

The result of this pragmatic defence was successful. The State did not appropriate any money of the Church of England for secular purposes. No plans for disestablishment were formulated; Church reform became the order of the day. It is not relevant here to examine these reforms but it is interesting to note that by 1840 Mill was disgusted with the line Parliament had taken and Arnold thought he had been mistaken about the extreme danger of the Church in 1832 which had prompted his pamphlet on Church reform. Yet it was a close thing in 1832 which the security of eight years later ought not to obscure. During those years Blomfield and Peel produced efficiency and Church Extension, a programme which Blomfield in particular prosecuted with unremitting vigour, and of which Shaftesbury was a critic because of the mission situation which, he said, confronted the Church.[13] However, the programme went on.

Such churches as there were in England were becoming increasingly separated from the mass of the population in the rapidly expanding towns, especially of the north.[14] Formerly the province of York had been both poor and underpopulated, with two thousand parishes and six bishoprics, compared with the ten thousand parishes of the province of Canterbury with its twenty bishoprics. Now

[13] O. J. Brose, op. cit., p. 206.

[14] Since 1688 little or no thought had been given by the Church to the building programme which the population might need. During the reign of Queen Anne an Act of Parliament had been passed for the building of churches but had never been implemented fully. Only ten out of fifty churches were built. In 1818 a grant of one million pounds was made, and to this further contributions were added by the Treasury and private donors. This money built the so-called "Waterloo Churches".

the north was growing in both population and wealth. The population as a whole had increased from twelve million in 1811 to sixteen and a half million in 1831 and it rose to twenty-one million in 1851. Sheffield increased in size from 35,840 in 1811 to 59,011 in 1831; and Manchester, Liverpool and Leeds rose in the same proportion, or greater. Neither Lancashire nor the West Riding, two areas of heaviest development, had their own bishop, until in 1836 the Church reformers created the diocese of Ripon for the West Riding and the diocese of Manchester in 1847 for Lancashire. The Ecclesiastical Commissioners also promoted the creation of many new parishes.

Despite this the new areas remained deficient not only in the provision of churches, but in free sittings where churches were provided. In Sheffield about 1821 "there were not three hundred sittings for the poor in all the churches (Established) of Sheffield".[15] Liverpool had pews for twenty-one thousand out of a population of ninety-four thousand; Manchester had only eleven thousand for seventy-nine thousand, even though a number of churches had been built since 1760. As Bishop Blomfield wrote: "It is the object of the Commissioners for building new churches, as far as they can, to intermingle the seats of the rich and the poor, so as to afford the latter nearly the same facilities for hearing which the former enjoy. We have found considerable difficulty in realizing our own wishes in that respect, on account of the objections which were made by the richer classes to too great an intermixture of the poor among them, objections which it was absolutely necessary to attend to because the whole income of the Minister depends on the new rents accruing exclusively from the richer classes."[16] This custom, which obtained not only in these

[15] Evidence of a Sheffield clergyman to a Royal Commission quoted in E. R. Wickham, *Church and People in an Industrial City,* Lutterworth, 1957, p. 70.

[16] Quoted in J. L. and B. Hammond, *The Bleak Age,* Pelican Books, 1947, p. 120.

new mission churches but also in many of the old parish churches, was deeply resented by the working classes as a whole and produced continual irritation and occasional demonstrations.

Arnold was an acute critic of many features of the new industrial society. His private correspondence, his letters to the *Sheffield Courant*[17] and the *Hertford Reformer,*[18] his sermons and the prefaces all show considerable insight into the changing shape of society and specially into the pressures upon the new industrial working class. Originally Arnold had set up his own weekly paper *The Englishman's Register* in 1831, "more to relieve his own conscience than with any sanguine hope of doing good", but "earnestly desiring to speak to the people the words of truth and soberness—to tell them plainly the evils that exist, and lead them, if I can, to their causes and their remedies".[19] His aim in the paper was "not the forwarding any political measure, but the so purifying, enlightening, sobering and, in one word, *Christianizing* men's notions and feelings on political matters, that from the improved tree may come hereafter a better fruit".[20] The paper died a natural death after a few weeks. However, he discovered that a number of his articles had been copied in the *Sheffield Courant* and he began a regular correspondence with its editor who published the letters in the paper; the first thirteen of which constitute the best exposition of his views, in the opinion of Dean Stanley, on the main causes of social distress in England.

[17] *The Miscellaneous Works of Thomas Arnold,* ed. A. P. Stanley, London, 1845, pp. 169-248. The *Sheffield Courant* appeared from 1793 to 1797, when it went bankrupt, under the motto, *Nolumus leges Angliae mutari*. It reappeared in 1827 under the editorship of J. C. Platt, who acquired Arnold's contributions for a further seven years.

[18] Op. cit., pp. 431-519.

[19] Stanley, op. cit., pp. 244-5. Extracts from *The Englishman's Register, 1831. Miscellaneous Works,* pp. 113-67.

[20] Stanley, op. cit., pp. 258-9.

He returned to the same theme in later years in his contributions to the *Hertford Reformer*. It might be argued that the letters are too general and lacking in particular applications to be of much service. Arnold himself was aware of this. He wrote: "What I sent them was, I knew, too general and discursive for a newspaper; but they would insert all my articles."[21] He also remarked : "My writing partakes of the character of my way of life, which is very much retired from the highway of politics, and of all great discussions."[22] He felt that the most he could do was to "pull the bell, as it were, and try to give the alarm as to the magnitude of the danger".[23] Such a warning was needed, not least by the Church. "It fills me with astonishment to see anti-slavery and missionary societies so busy with the ends of the earth, and yet all the worst evils of slavery and of heathenism are existing amongst ourselves. But no man seems so gifted, or to speak more properly so endowed by God with the spirit of wisdom, as to read this fearful riddle truly; which most Sphinx-like, if not read truly, will most surely be the destruction of us all".[24]

In both series of letters he points to the miseries of the new industrial population. The working classes were legally free men, but in fact they were treated as slaves. "This then is the great evil in the condition of a manufacturing population, that it implies the congregation of a vast multitude within a comparatively narrow space, and with an object purely commercial. In other words they are regarded as *hands*—not as heads, hearts or souls. . . ."[25] Arnold was particularly sensitive to the affront to human dignity in the new factory system, both in the factory and in the neighbourhoods which the workers inhabited. These localities were miserable. "Now consider the appearance of a manufacturing town or village. There is the great manufactory, and there are the long rows of cottages which constitute the

[21] Ibid., p. 460. [22] Ibid., p. 460. [23] Ibid., p. 531.
[24] Ibid., p. 489. [25] *Miscellaneous Works*, p. 456.

dwellings of the poor manufacturing workmen. Besides there are some poor shops supplying such articles as the workmen require; and perhaps, but not always, there would be the houses of the clergyman and the doctor. But these are lost amidst the multitude of the poor."[26]

This was life based on a commercial and not on a community relationship. It was a common idea that leisure was a snare to the working classes; some notable theologians had taught the necessity of industrious lives to banish sin. Amenities for refreshment of body, mind, and spirit were lacking. Sheffield was almost destitute of open places. In 1844 Preston alone had a public park. When Lord Stamford threw open his park on a Sunday the workpeople from Manchester flocked there, and though twenty thousand visited it no damage was done. Memories of country life were still alive in the manufacturing towns of the north. The lack of "common enjoyment" (to use the Hammonds' phrase) was serious for a class used to the countryside and its rough field sports. Monotony of environment and of work produced "accidie". There were neither libraries, nor cheap concerts, nor other entertainments to revive their spirits. The tavern was the only solace. Even the parochial life of the Church shut them out from refreshment by its drab exclusiveness. As to housing, this was no new problem. Dirt and stench were normal. Attempts at improvement during the eighteenth century were largely ineffective; there was little significant advance until the arrival of cheap water and sewerage. What made this chronic situation even worse was the rapid growth of towns and the increased movement of labour, which created an acute need for more houses, many of which were constructed badly. Perhaps the housing ought not to be thought of too darkly, and certainly the pitiful cellar dwellings of Manchester ought not to be taken as typical. "A working man of good standard lived in a house with three or four rooms and a kitchen, and on the whole

[26] Op. cit., p. 458.

the standard was rising with the extension of the skilled trades."[27] Yet the lack of amenities remained to be remedied but slowly.

In 1831 Arnold attributed "our present distress" among other causes to "the long war which raged through Europe for more than twenty years, everywhere deranging the state of society, and in England forcing suddenly the increase of our population and of our commerce and manufacture to an unnatural and therefore mischievous excess . . ." and also to "the natural tendency of wealth to become richer, and of poverty to become poorer; by which trade carried on a large scale has driven trade on a smaller scale out of the market".[28] This not only created new social relationships but upset old relationships; a widening gap appeared between farmers and their labourers—farmers "take no more notice of them *than if they were dumb beasts*".[29]

In the midst of these developments there was the growth of an indigenous working-class society, of which Arnold was not entirely approving. "Being thus without the organization of regular society, the organization which they have among themselves is rather mischievous than beneficial—they are formed into clubs and unions—associations which breathe a narrow and selfish spirit at the best, but which, under favourable circumstances, become mere gangs of conspirators; the isolation in which they exist, with respect to the larger national society around them, being apt in a moment to become alienation and active hostility."[30] Arnold's fear was a Jacobin revolution on the French model. If industrialism created a slave society, there would be an explosion, engineered by the slaves' leaders. "We see a slave rebellion breaking out—or a burning just below the surface, over a large part of the kingdom."[31] Chartism represented this slave rebellion to Arnold: "When I hear the

[27] E. L. Woodward, *The Age of Reform, 1815-1870,* p. 10.
[28] *Miscellaneous Works,* pp. 175-6.
[29] Op. cit., p. 178. [30] Ibid., p. 462. [31] Ibid., p. 492.

Chartist leaders talk with indifference or with hatred of all our old institutions—when I find them perfectly ignorant and careless of history, and as incapable of carrying forward their views beyond the immediate present, I see again the certain marks of slaves—I hear a language which in all but slaves is insanity."[32] Arnold was not sentimental about the working class although he understood and sympathized with their sufferings. His suspicion of working class leadership is easily explicable at a time preceding the existence of a national police force and universal education and less than two generations after the French Revolution. But he stood firmly for educating and raising the standard of living of the working class.

Arnold was no friend of Conservatism. In 1835 he wrote to Mr Justice Coleridge: "I think . . . that Conservatism is always wrong; so thoroughly wrong in principle, that, even when the particular reform proposed may be by no means the best possible, yet it is good as a triumph over Conservatism. . . . I think Conservatism far worse than Toryism, if by Toryism be meant a fondness for monarchial or even despotic government . . . but Conservatism always looks backwards, and therefore under whatever form of government, I think it the enemy of all good."[33]

Arnold partly attributed the troubles of the times "to the excess of aristocracy in our whole system, religious, political and social; an evil arising from causes which run back to the earliest period of our history; and which have tended silently and unconsciously to separate the higher classes from the lower in almost every relation of life".[34] Arnold thought that the territorial aristocracy, checked from abuses of its power by the new merchant class, should make a con-

[32] Ibid., p. 492.

[33] Stanley, p. 391. Sir John Taylor Coleridge, 1790-1876, nephew of S. T. Coleridge; called to the bar, 1819; frequent contributor to the *Quarterly Review*; editor of Blackstone's *Commentaries*, 1825; Recorder of Exeter, 1832; King's Bench, 1835-1858; Privy Councillor, 1858.

[34] *Miscellaneous Works*, p. 175.

scious effort to narrow this gulf and thus exercise responsible leadership in politics and education. He hoped that the aristocracy would join working class organizations, be ready to admit previous faults and to provide alternative leadership to working class agitators, and so prepare the working class to use parliamentary reform in a responsible manner, somewhat on the pattern of British colonial policy, which so many of Arnold's pupils subsequently administered.

Arnold stood against revolution and conservatism, and for reform in all spheres.[35] His remarks on equality indicate his approach. "Our business is to raise all, and to lower none. Equality is the dream of a madman, or the passion of a fiend. Extreme inequality, or higher comfort and civilization in some, co-existing with deep misery and degradation in others, is no less a folly and a sin."[36] In pursuit of reform Arnold was not prepared to put all his hope in one solution. Each proposed reform had some limited use. Parliamentary reform and reform of the Poor Law (both of which Arnold supported), the extension of education, work for the new University of London and the Mechanics' Institutes show how his concern for education went beyond his own life's work at Rugby school. Arnold saw that some immediate needs would be met by a new deal in the local government of industrial areas, "the subdivision of parishes and townships, so as to furnish to every thousand of human beings the benefits of what may really be called society".[37] Yet the malaise of society went deeper; the system called in question the meaning of politics—the purpose of society, its goals, and thus its relation with the Church.

[35] Arnold's attitude to University reform is characteristic: "No man ought to meddle with the Universities who does not know them well and love them well; they are great and noble places—and I am sure that no man in England has a deeper affection for Oxford than I have, or more appreciates its inimitable advantages. And therefore I wish it improved and reformed—though this is a *therefore* which men are exceedingly slow to understand." Stanley, p. 443.

[36] Op. cit., p. 182.

[37] Ibid., p. 499.

3

CHRISTIAN POLITICS AND IDENTITY OF CHURCH AND STATE

"WE must remember how the Greek Science, πολιτική, of which the English word "politics", or even political science, is so inadequate a translation—society in its connection with the highest welfare of men—exhibited to him the great problem which every educated man was called upon to solve", so Stanley wrote in his *Life of Arnold*.[1] The seriousness with which Arnold treated politics emerges, for example, in his last letter to the *Hertford Reformer*. "What I wish for above all things, is that men would talk, write, and act on political subjects, in the fear of God; as if they were forthwith going to stand before His judgement."[2] The posthumous *Fragments on Church and State* contains plans of works on Christian politics, dating from 1827 and 1833: "I have long had in mind a work on Christian Politics, or the application of the Gospel to the state of man as a citizen."[3]

Arnold held a high view of the State. He opposed the view that the State should hold the ring in the economic struggle: "The very name of society implies that it shall not be a mere race, but that its object is to provide for the common good of all, by restraining the power of the strong and protecting the helplessness of the weak."[4] He opposed "that wretched doctrine of Warburton's that the State had

[1] Stanley, p. 194.

[2] *Miscellaneous Works*, pp. 517-8.

[3] Op. cit., London, 1845, p. 6.

[4] *Miscellaneous Works*, p. 454.

only to look after body and goods".[5] In *The Alliance between Church and State* Warburton had said that the end of civil society "is no other than security to the temporal liberty and property of Man".[6] Arnold wrote: "The State has a far nobler end than the care of men's bodies and goods."[7] It was concerned with a moral end—the improvement of mankind.

This was an eschatological view of the State in that this end was not to be achieved in the foreseeable future or in terms of this mortal life. Arnold wrote in 1831: "I have not the slightest expectation of what is commonly called the Millennium, and I wonder more and more that anyone can so understand Scripture as to look for it. As for the signs of the times in England, I look nowhere with confidence."[8] Yet this did not deter Arnold from working for partial realization of the State's aims. As he wrote to Archbishop Whately about his own scheme of Church reform: "though it will never be wholly realized, yet if men can be brought to look at it as the true theory, the practical approximations to it may be in the course of time indefinitely great."[9]

In the State the individual had his place and rights, but the State was a corporation larger than the individual with greater claims than the individual. Arnold wrote in the *Fragments on Church and State*: "We hear a great deal too much in the present day of the political rights of *individuals*; this tendency, which is not essentially anarchical, is one of the most distinguishing features of modern civilization as distinguished from that of the ancient world. The

[5] Stanley, p. 501.

[6] Op. cit., Bk. I, ch. 4. *The Alliance* was written to assert the "Necessity and Equity of Established Religion and a Test Law", but it sets out Church and State as separate bodies, with different aims on different levels, but requiring the co-operation of each other for the attainment of these aims.

[7] *Miscellaneous Works*, p. 466.

[8] Stanley, p. 266.

[9] Ibid., p. 201. Richard Whately, 1787-1863; Fellow of Oriel, 1811, and Archbishop of Dublin, 1831.

age of chivalry, whose departure Burke so much regretted, was in one respect the natural parent of that age of Jacobinism which he so much abhorred. Both breathe the spirit of lawlessness, encouraging men to look upon themselves as independent of their fellows; cultivating a proud and selfish idolatry of what belongs to them individually, whether it be personal honour, and personal glory, as the earlier form of the disease, or personal political liberty and equality as in the later. Both lead to what Bacon calls *bonum suitatis,* to the neglect of the good of the whole body of which we are members. Individuals, in a political sense, are necessarily members; as distinct from the body, they are nothing. Against society, they have no political rights whatever, and their belonging to society or not is a matter not of their own choice, but determined for them by their being born and bred members of it."[10] A disruptive individualism has been a feature of middle class culture in industrial society, and Arnold was aware of its political origins.

The aims and purposes of the State confined men in certain ways. The individual should profess the State's religion. "To those who think that political society was ordained for higher purposes than those of mere politics or of traffic, the principle of the ancient commonwealths in making agreement in religion and morals the test of citizenship cannot but appear wise and good."[11] For this reason Arnold was against giving Jews full citizenship.

Christianity was in a special sense the bond of society, because Church and State shared the same moral ends. "It so happens that the subject of conformity, of communion, of the relations of Church and State, of Church Government, etc., is one which I have studied more than any other which I could name."[12] Arnold wrote in 1833, justifying his pamphlet on Church reform. To Bunsen in 1838 he wrote:

[10] Op. cit., pp. 52-3.

[11] *Miscellaneous Works,* p. 395 (from the Preface to the Third Volume of Thucydides).

[12] Stanley, p. 302.

"Now I want to know what principles and objects a Christian state can have, if it be really Christian, more or less than those of the Church. In whatever degree it differs from the Church, it becomes, I think, in that exact proportion, unchristian. In short, it seemed to me that the state must be 'the world' if it be not 'the Church', but for a society of Christians to be 'the world' seems monstrous."[13] In 1840 he wrote: "I look to the full development of the Christian Church in its perfect form, as the Kingdom of God, for the most effective removal of all evils, and promotion of all good, and I can understand no perfect Church or perfect State, without their blending into one in this ultimate form."[14] In this Arnold holds the theory of the two sides of the coin: the English people from the political point of view are the English State or nation, from the religious point of view the English Church or the Church of England. They are the same people organized in two different ways.

The identity of Church and State rested upon the doctrine of the King's Supremacy, "the very cornerstone of all my political belief". Arnold wrote: "I am equally opposed to Popery, High Churchism, and the claims of the Scotch Presbyteries, on the one hand; and to all the Independents, and advocates of the separation, as they call it, of Church and State, on the other; the first setting up a Priesthood in the place of the Church, and the other lowering necessarily the objects of Law and Government, and reducing them to a mere system of police, while they profess to wish to make the Church purer."[15] In the *Fragments on Church and State* Arnold wrote: "By God's blessing we in England have rec-

[13] Ibid., pp. 496-7. Christian Charles Josias, Baron von Bunsen, 1791-1860; married an Englishwoman; secretary to Niebuhr, while the latter was Prussian ambassador in Rome; Prussian ambassador in Berne, 1840; ambassador in London, 1842-1854, where he was Frederick William IV's agent in establishing the Jerusalem bishopric; baron, 1857. His *Zeichen der Zeit,* 1855, helped to revive the liberal movement in Germany after its post-1848 setbacks.

[14] Ibid., p. 535.

[15] Ibid., p. 535.

ognized, although rather by a provincial overruling of our purposes than from a consciousness on our part of its full value, that great doctrine which is at once negative and positive; which, not content with denying and exposing falsehood, offers to us in the place of the falsehood so destroyed that divine truth in which is contained all goodness. This doctrine is that of the King's Supremacy;—which while it puts down the false claims of the pretended apostolical succession on the one hand, denies no less firmly on the other hand the notion that the State has only to look after men's bodies and goods. It declared the identity of the Church and State, when each has attained to its perfection; both desire to effect man's greatest good; but the Church during her imperfect state is deficient in power: the State in the like condition is deficient in knowledge: one judges amiss of man's highest happiness; the other discerns it truly, but has not the power on a large scale to attain it. But when blended into one, the power and knowledge become happily united; the Church is become sovereign, and the State has become Christian."[16]

This identity of Church and State meant that religious questions are also political, and political questions religious. The clergy have a political and educational rôle in society; Arnold drew frequently upon S. T. Coleridge's ideas. "The clergy of a national Church are directly called upon to Christianize the nation: not only to inculcate the private virtues of the Gospel but its pure and holy principles in their full extent; those divine laws of which it may indeed be said that their voice is the harmony of the world."[17] Par-

[16] Op. cit., pp. 98-9.

[17] Ibid., Appendix I. "Arnold was deeply influenced by Coleridge, above all by his 'Constitution of Church and State'; in him the Coleridgean 'Ideas' became a programme of action." B. Willey, *Nineteenth Century Studies,* London, Chatto and Windus, 1949, p. 49. "I think, with all his faults, old Sam was more of a great man than any one who has lived within the four seas in my memory" (Arnold to Hull, 16 November 1836), Stanley, p. 424.

liament and the legal system have a religious and moral rôle in promoting the moral ends of society.

This identity also removes any false distinction between sacred and secular. No political question ceases to be religious—politics in the fear of God—and no religious question is purely for religious specialists. "I cannot understand", Arnold wrote, "what is the good of a national Church if it be not to Christianize the Nation, and introduce the principles of Christianity into men's social and civil relations, and expose the wickedness of that spirit which maintains the game laws, and in agriculture and trade seems to think that there is no such sin as covetousness, and that if a man is not dishonest he has nothing to do but to make all the profit of his capital that he can."[18] "There is a certain reluctance amongst many who are very zealous supporters of the outward establishment of Christianity, to admitting its principles in the concerns of common life, in matters belonging to their trade or profession or above all in the conduct of national affairs. They will not tolerate its spirit in their everyday practice but ridicule it as visionary and impracticable."[19]

From the perspective of the twentieth century Bishop Gore, a shrewd commentator upon the social history of the Church, saw this to be the major fault of the Church during the Industrial Revolution. In *Christ and Society* he wrote of the Industrial Revolution "as a period of collapse and failure, because the Church was content to abdicate from the function of applying the principles of brotherhood to the relations of men and nations, and to witness without remonstrance the establishment of the quite alien principle of selfish competition as dominant in these great fields of human activity".[20]

The distinction between sacred and secular, "striking as

[18] Stanley, p. 243.
[19] *Sermons,* 7th edition, 1861, p. vi.
[20] Op. cit., London, 1928, p. 133.

with a two-edged sword, and pulling asunder what God had joined, made common life profane and religious life formal and superstitious: for what are all our business and our studies but profane, if not done in Christ's name? and what are our acts of religion but the extremest folly and falsehood, if they are not made to act upon our common life? Every act of a Christian is at once secular and sacred".[21] In the sphere of moral philosophy the distinction is untenable. "If I take no notice of the authority and influences of Christianity, I unavoidably take a view of man's life and principles from which they are excluded, that is a view which acknowledged some other authority and influence—it may be of some other religion, or of some philosophy, or of mere common opinion or instinct—but in any case, I have one of many views of life and conduct which it was the very purpose of Christ's coming to exclude. And how can any Christian man lend himself to the propagating or sanctioning a system of moral knowledge which assumes that Christ's law is not our rule, nor His promise our motive of action?"[22]

Arnold's theory of Church and State is open to criticism. In the first place he can be charged with ignoring economics. Gloyn says: "In his theory of the Christian state, he exhibited the same weakness as Coleridge. Both men failed to recognize that a solution of the problems of the time required a change in the economic arrangements of society and that a solution could not be expected from moral and intellectual enlightenment alone or from a philosophy of *noblesse oblige*."[23] It is true that Arnold analyses the social relationships of the new industrial society and not the economic ones and that his analysis is therefore incomplete, but he recognizes that the new industrial working class has

[21] *Miscellaneous Works,* pp. 473-4. [22] Stanley, p. 444.

[23] C. K. Gloyn, *The Church in the Social Order,* Pacific University, 1942, p. 109. Gloyn's chapter on Arnold is one of the best studies and summaries of his ideas.

cause for complaint and his theory of a nation in which all have a community of interest is good. Arnold's solution lies in the spread of education rather than in a change of economic structure.

Another criticism of Arnold lies in the excessive power that he would allow to government. In these days of massive totalitarian governments with control of the means of communication and repression there is something to be said for Warburton and the State holding the ring. Arnold wrote at a time when many of the urgent reforms could only be carried out by a central authority which was reluctant to take power to itself and when many of the abuses requiring reform were the products of individualism rampant in Church and State. In the 1830's the case for religious and political pluralism was at a discount. To recreate the Hookerian ideal with a comprehensive National Church and a political body with a strong central government was to arrive at the opposite pole from pluralism, which in its religious aspect appeared to Arnold to be destroying the Church and in its political aspect appeared to be tolerating great social evils. Subsequent history has seen in England a sort of semi-pluralism: in religion an Established Church in a far from dominating position with strong Free Church and Roman Catholic rivals and in politics an increase of central power with strong countervailing groups in local government, industry, and education. That Arnold could accommodate himself to this situation is suggested by the fact that he had reservations before he died about his own monolithic theory of Church and State. "I am myself so much inclined to the idea of a strong social bond, that I ought not to be suspected of any tendency to anarchy; yet I am beginning to think that the idea may be overstrained, and that this attempt to merge the soul and will of the individual in the general body is, when fully developed, contrary to the very essence of Christianity." Stanley says the epistles of Cyprian, for example, indicated to Arnold "that the Church had been corrupted, not only by the Judaic spirit of priesthood, but even more by the Gentile spirit of government, stifling the sense of individual responsibility."[24]

[24] Stanley, p. 608.

4

FAILURE OF THE CHURCH

THE international character of the Church had become increasingly weak by the end of the Middle Ages; at the Reformation most countries in Western Europe had developed a strongly national consciousness. The parliaments of Henry VIII had declared England to be an empire and asserted the common headship of the monarch over all departments of the national life. The notion of National Churches had emerged identified with the countries in which they were situated, yet part of the Catholic Church. "As the common sea possesses the name of many oceans," wrote Hooker, "so does the Church." At the same time, "Seeing there is not any man of the Church of England but the same is also a member of the Commonwealth, nor any man a member of the Commonwealth which is not also of the Church of England; . . . so albeit properties and actions of one kind do cause the name of a commonwealth, qualities and functions of another sort the name of a Church to be given unto a multitude, yet one and the selfsame multitude may in such sort be both, and is so with us, that no person appertaining to the one can be denied to be also of the other".[1] With this notion of a National Church comprehending the life of the whole nation Arnold had great sympathy, even though he disliked parts of the *Laws of Ecclesiastical Polity* on account of Hooker's love of "priestly and ceremonial religion such as appears in the Fifth Book".[2]

[1] Hooker, *Laws of Ecclesiastical Polity,* VIII, i, 2.

[2] Stanley, p. 430.

In his *Principles of Church Reform* Arnold outlined the purpose of a national establishment of religion which was to Christianize the total life of the nation in the nineteenth century. The Church ought to be concerned with the entire social life of the country, "For", wrote Hooker, "pure and unstained religion ought to be the highest of all cares appertaining to public regiment",[3] and "all true virtues are to honour true religion as their parent and all well-ordered commonwealths to love her as their chiefest stay".[4] In the midst of profound changes in the early nineteenth century such an outlook was vital. It had a bearing upon ideas of a neutral or secular state, common among the liberals, and upon attitudes towards tithes, church maintenance, and extension. Yet in the face of existing dissenting opposition such a national appeal could hardly be justified. This, thought Arnold, was "entirely at the bottom of our difficulties in this way". "We can never get on consistently and smoothly till something be done to try and remedy this."[5] If churches, for instance, could be regarded as "public buildings for a national object" a minority could not object to maintaining them. "If they are only to be maintained by those who belong to one religious denomination it strikes, of course, at the very root of any Establishment, because the same principle must apply equally to tithes."[6]

"The 'Idea' of my life, to which I think every thought of my mind more or less tends, is the perfecting the 'idea' of the Edward the Sixth Reformers,—the constructing a truly National and Christian Church."[7] But this grand idea of the identity of Christian Nation and National Church, governed in all departments by Christian politics was sadly decayed in Arnold's time. He feared that the time had now come "when evils long neglected, and good long omitted, will have brought things to such a state, that the constitution must fall to save the commonwealth, and the Church

[3] Hooker, V, i, 2. [4] Ibid., V, i, 5. [5] Stanley, p. 557.
[6] Ibid., p. 433. [7] Ibid., p. 386.

of England perish for the sake of the Church of Christ".[8]

In 1835 Arnold wrote: "But now, the true and grand idea of a Church, that is, a society for the purpose of making men like Christ,—earth like heaven,—the kingdoms of this world the Kingdom of Christ,—is all lost; and men look upon it as 'an institution for religious instruction and religious worship', thus robbing it of its life and universality, making it an affair of clergy, not of people—of preaching and ceremonies, not of living—of Sundays and synagogues, instead of one of all days and all places, houses, streets, towns and country."[9]

IN MISSION TO AN INDUSTRIAL SOCIETY

In the early nineteenth century the Church of England was far from being the Church of the Nation. The idea of the Establishment was attacked, its benefits misunderstood. "The most general complaint against the Church turns upon the excessive amount, and the unequal distribution of its property, and especially upon the burdensome and impolitic nature of the tithe system. There is also a strong popular feeling against the political opinions of the clergy, particularly of the bishops and other dignitaries among them."[10]

The failure of the Church itself was a cause of irreligion. "In many cases the real origin of a man's irreligion is, I believe, political. He dislikes the natural state of society, hates the Church as connected with it, and, in his notions, supporting its abuses, and then hates Christianity because it is taught by the Church."[11]

The notable studies of J. L. and Barbara Hammond express well the extent to which the traditional forms of religion of the time belonged to an older order of society and were alien to the new industrial working class. "Religion

[8] Ibid., p. 354.
[9] Ibid., pp. 387-8.
[10] *Miscellaneous Works*, p. 219.
[11] Stanley, p. 272.

was, in fact, part of the civil constitution of society. The English Church accepted that position. It knew its place in the domestic establishment of the State, and it took its colour for good and for evil from the world of the ruling class.

"The working classes had no use for this religion. They did not find themselves in a world of congenial occupation, with leisure graced by art and literature, rounded off by the polite worship of reasonableness and moderation that chose to call itself Christianity. Life did not seem to them the simple flow of satisfactory and sensible consequences from satisfactory and sensible causes. For them, as a great scholar said of the age of Marcus Aurelius, 'Le monde s'attristait'. Many things existed or happened that called for an explanation or a protest. Moreover, while the ruling class looked with composure on a civilization that they guided, elegant masters of their world, the working classes were conscious of an overwhelming burden in the mass and power of the forces that seemed to hold them captive, and to reduce their place in the scheme of the universe to one of mean and helpless insignificance. A religion that tended to be a little more than a religion of manners, teaching its adherents to admire the framework of a world made and ordered by a Providence of good taste and discreet conduct, offered neither explanation nor consolation in the depths of the mine or the heat and rage of the furnace."[12]

The Hammonds point out, as Arnold well appreciated, that reform of abuses alone would not solve the problem of creating a new expression of religion. "It was one thing to put an end to sinecures and abuses and to give a serious and responsible character to the office of the parsons, hitherto regarded and held with such levity; it was another to satisfy the imagination of the great population on whose daily life of bleak and monotonous toil those civilizing in-

[12] J. L. and B. Hammond, *The Town Labourer, 1760-1832,* Guild Books, 1949, vol. II, pp. 99-100.

fluences to which mankind has looked for comfort, ever since the first city found shelter behind its encircling walls, shed so pale and doubtful a light."[13]

Hensley Henson in an essay on "The Church of England" in *Church Problems* quotes some interesting though extreme judgements. "There is no church that is so completely and thoroughly as the Anglican the product and expression of the wants and wishes, the modes of thought and cast of character, not of a certain nationality, but of a fragment of a nation, namely, the rich, fashionable and cultivated classes." ". . . Anglicanism has always been the religion of the educated classes exclusively. It has never at any period been national and popular, because it implies more historical information and a wider political horizon than can be possessed by the peasant or the artisan. The masses require an intuitional religion, such as is provided by the grosser forms of Dissent in Great Britain."[14]

The failure of the Church was most noticeable in the new industrial areas. Arnold wrote to the *Sheffield Courant,* before the Reform Bill was passed: "Hear the cry with which the bishops in particular are now assailed in every part of the kingdom, and most loudly in the great manufacturing districts. Whence comes the especial bitterness with which they, above all other anti-reforming peers, are everywhere attacked? Whence the hatred with which the whole order of the clergy is sometimes pursued? Is it not because the people have never been made to feel the full amount of the good which an Established Church may and ought to effect, and therefore are the more ready to complain of its endowments? Is it not because in our large manufacturing towns the Church has allowed thousands and tens of thousands of its members to grow up in misery

[13] J. L. and B. Hammond, *The Bleak Age,* Pelican Books, 1947, p. 118.

[14] Op. cit., John Murray, 1900, pp. 1-2. The quotations are from Döllinger in 1862 and Mark Pattison in 1863.

and in ignorance; and that a step-mother's neglect is naturally requited by something of a step-mother's unpopularity?

". . . The reproach attaches itself to the body. What worse than folly was its talk of delicacies, and difficulties, and the danger of Parliamentary interferences, and the mischief of interfering with Church property, when the very end for which the establishment existed was left unattained? Was it fit to wait for money enough to build an expensive church, rather than licence the first room, or the first courtyard that could be found, wherever the inhabitants of the parish became too numerous or too remote to attend the parish church? Was it even decent to leave many thousand persons to the instruction and care of one minister, rather than apply to Parliament for power to make a new allotment of the Church property, such as the new state of things required?"[15] "Indeed when we consider the utter inadequacy of the Establishment, as it now stands, to meet the wants of the great manufacturing towns and districts, it may be said that in those portions of the kingdom our business is not so much to reform the Church, as to create one."[16] Thus the Church had ignored, and failed to adapt its structure to the new industrial populations, which to a great extent were unchurched. A large section of the English nation was outside any church, including the Dissenting bodies.

In Separation from the Dissenters

The Dissenters themselves were a further sign of the failure of the Church of England to organize Englishmen into a single Christian body. The seventeenth-century attempts at comprehension had not succeeded. The Act of Toleration was a recognition of the fact of division and the

[15] *Miscellaneous Works,* pp. 210-11.

[16] Ibid., p. 337; see also p. 168.

eighteenth century settled down to live comfortably with it. "The whole tendency of the last century, and of men's minds now, is to shun all notions of comprehension; as the knot was once cut by persecution, so it is to be cut now by toleration and omission."[17] In the postscript to the pamphlet on Church Reform Arnold wrote: "I should rather say that the founders of the Protestant Church of England considered them (Church and State) as identical:—the Christian nation of England was the Church of England:—the head of that nation was for that very reason the head of the Church:—the public officers of the nation, whether civil or ecclesiastical were officers therefore of the Church:—and every Englishman was supposed to be properly a member of it. . . . Is it indifference or latitudinarianism to wish most devoutedly that this noble, this divine theory may be fully and for ever realized?

"It is owing to the existence of religious dissent that not only is it not realized in practice, but its very truth and excellence are disputed. And that dissent has arisen out of faults and errors on both sides, on the part of the Dissenters no less than on that of the Church, is a fact which no impartial man can doubt."[18]

A Church divided into sects was failing to perform its primary essential duties, because the existence of Dissent in England had so divided the efforts of Christians as to make them more adverse to each other, rather than to the cause of ungodliness and wickedness.

For more than two centuries Dissent had been a powerful ferment in English society with its appeal to the right of private judgement and its defence of tender consciences. The Elizabethan "Classical" Presbyterian system and the Brownists had been the first expression of this, by which the unity of the nation was rent, and the division made permanent at the Restoration, in 1660. From then on there

[17] Stanley, p. 445.
[18] *Miscellaneous Works*, pp. 335-7; see also pp. 166-7.

were numerous suggestions how to produce a National Church but none of them came to anything. The Independents and the Baptists were totally irreconcilable; the Presbyterians faded away rapidly towards the end of the century and after the collapse of the Comprehension Bill of 1689, the notion of toleration took its place. A large measure of toleration came, in practice, to be granted, which allowed the Dissenters to take a prominent part in public life. The Evangelical Revival injected fresh life into this old Dissent and by the turn of the eighteenth century a new situation had arisen in which a new religious society, the Methodists, had been born and in which the total number of dissenting chapels outnumbered the churches of the Establishment, and probably equalled it in active support. One of the immediate causes of Arnold's pamphlet on Church Reform was the pressure of Dissent against the Established Church.

In Arnold's eyes the Church had failed in its missionary task and failed to realize unity. He understood mission in a wider sense to include not only the provision of religious organization and facilities for the new populations but also a civilizing, educational task; his view of mission was intensive as well as extensive. To Arnold comprehension was not only the road to unity but unity itself. Through comprehension in terms of the nineteenth century the ideal of a National Church could be realized.

In its Internal Life

The Church's internal life also bore the marks of this double failure. Inevitably its structure could not reflect the structure of the nation. The Church did not embrace the whole nation, but even the part which it did embrace was not reflected in its structure. Its ministry tended to be aristocratic and movements of vitality such as the Oxford Movement, of which Arnold was a discerning critic, tended to become a religious preserve of specialists. Sectarianism was a great evil to Arnold; he saw it in the Oxford Movement, which appeared to be creating a sharp division between sacred and secular, narrowing the Church down to a simple identification with the priesthood and converting the National Church into a sect. It was a mark of sectarians to turn religion and its practices into ends in themselves; this Arnold attacked. "Religious instruction, the exercises of prayer and praise, the participation in the sacraments, are amongst the prescribed and most necessary means for our growth in goodness. Still it is most essential that they should always be clearly seen to be means, and not in themselves an end; that their bearing is upon human life and character; that they belong to the Church of Christ as instruments, and that the Church was founded not merely for the perfecting those instruments, but for their application after being perfected; that its members should worship together, in order to live together; and that their combined efforts are wanted, not only for sowing the seed, but for cherishing the plant and reaping the harvest; that the Church, in short, is more for the week-days than for the Sunday; more for the house, street, or the field, than for that particular building which, by an unfortunate ambiguity of language, has appropriated to itself its name."[19]

Arnold's dissatisfaction with the internal life, structure, and direction of the Church may be illustrated by his views on two subjects, the order of deacons and the Oxford Movement. A revival of the order of deacons was a small item in the revival of the Church; and the Oxford Movement did not mean the destruction of the Church. Yet his views on both bring out in some detail what Arnold considered to be important and what unimportant in the life of the Church.

[19] *Fragments on Church and State*, pp. 25-6.

The Ministry and the Order of Deacons

"You are entering on an office extinct in all but name", Arnold wrote to Stanley on his ordination to the diaconate. "If it could be revived in power, it would be one of the greatest blessings that could be conferred on the Church!"[20]

Earlier in 1839 Arnold had written more fully to Stanley advocating the revival of the order of deacons. A sermon preached in December 1839 in Rugby Parish Church developed the theme. Arnold mentioned it again in a letter to the *Hertford Reformer* in February 1840.

In May 1840 Arnold wrote to Chevalier Bunsen that he had signed a petition for alteration in the subscription to the Liturgy and Articles. "But for my own satisfaction, I drew up and sent to Whately a sketch of what I should myself wish to petition for; namely, the abolition of those political services for the 30th January, etc., and the repeal of all acts and canons which forbid deacons from following a secular calling. Sir R. Inglis is going to propose a grant of £400,000 a year for new clergymen; but surely his end would be better answered, and at no expense, by reviving the order of deacons. . . . Whately approved entirely of the petition, but thought it too abrupt a way of proceeding, as the subject would be new to so many."[21] The volume of

[20] Stanley, p. 526.

[21] Ibid., pp. 559-60.

(1) Of the political services one still is attached to the Book of Common Prayer; a special service for the day of the Sovereign's Accession. Three others were removed in 1859; those for 5 November, in memory of Gunpowder Treason or the Papists' conspiracy, 29 May in memory of the birth and return of Charles II, and 30 January a fast day in memory of the death of Charles I.

(2) Sir R. Inglis was Tory M.P. for Oxford, 1829-1854. He published as a pamphlet his House of Commons speech of 30 June 1840 on Church Extension.

(3) Whately himself presented a petition for alterations to the Prayer Book and Articles to the House of Lords on

Arnold's miscellaneous works contains a short paper on the order of deacons,[22] which according to Stanley, its editor, was circulated among Arnold's friends in 1841, and which may be the basis of the petition Arnold sent to Whately. Also in 1841 Arnold wrote the polemical introduction to the fourth volume of his sermons, *Christian Life, its Course, etc.*, which includes the Rugby Parish Church sermon of 1839.

In earlier writings on the reform of Church government Arnold had given his strongest argument for the revival of the diaconate, that of providing an adequate ordained ministry for the new industrial areas.

The paper on deacons begins: "The want of a sufficient number of ministers of the Church is more or less felt everywhere; but in large towns and in the extensive and populous parishes of the manufacturing districts, it is a most serious evil."[23] In the pamphlet on Church reform he commented that "the Church is like an army destitute of non-commissioned officers".[24]

Arnold's thinking about the diaconate began in the missionary and pastoral needs of the new industrial areas and developed in controversy with the Tractarians over the nature of the Church. He attacked the Tractarians for, in effect, confining the Church to the priesthood and for undermining its full, corporate nature. "There is no one abuse of the Romish system which may not be traced to the original and very early error of drawing a wide distinction between the clergy and the laity; of investing the former in such a peculiar degree with the attributes of the Church, that at last they retained them almost exclusively. In other

---

26 May 1840. The petition and some of the speeches in the debate are to be found in *Remains of the Most Reverend Charles Dickinson, D.D., Lord Bishop of Meath,* London, B. Fellowes, 1845, pp. 353-83; see also p. 171 n. 12.

[22] *Miscellaneous Works*, pp. 425-9.

[23] Ibid., p. 427.

[24] Ibid., p. 288; see also p. 117.

words, the great evil of popery is, that it has destroyed the Christian Church, and has substituted a priesthood in its room. . . . The real evils of the system are of a far older date than the supremacy of the Bishop of Rome, and exist in places where that supremacy is resolutely denied."[25] The Church is "narrowed still further by the practical extinction of one of the first orders of the clergy itself".[26] Therefore, "the first step towards the restoration of the Church seems to be the revival of the order of deacons".[27] Arnold argued that by allowing deacons to follow secular callings "a link would be formed between the clergy and the laity by the existence of an order partaking of the character of both. The confusion of confining the term Church to the clergy would be greatly dispelled: inasmuch as there would be not only members but even ministers of the Church who did not belong to the clergy considered as a profession."[28] Arnold ended his letter to Stanley, February 1839: "I have long thought that some plan of this sort might be the small end of the wedge, by which Anti-Christ might hereafter be burst asunder like the Dragon of Bel's temple."[29]

A revival of the diaconate would open the ministry to men who otherwise could not enter it. "The ministry of the Church would thus be safely and most beneficially open to persons of inferior rank and fortune, who cannot afford the expense of a university education, and have no prospects of a maintenance by entering the ministry as a profession, but who may have gifts which enable them to serve the Church effectually, and who may naturally and lawfully wish not to let these gifts lie idle."[30] In a letter to the *Hertford Reformer* Arnold instances "such good men . . . as do now after a manner supply the deacon's place in

[25] *Sermons, Christian Life, Its Course, Its Hindrances, and Its Helps,* 1842, pp. 418-9.

[26] Ibid., p. 414.

[27] Ibid., p. lxiv.

[28] *Miscellaneous Works,* p. 428.

[29] Stanley, p. 503.

[30] *Miscellaneous Works,* p. 428.

large towns, under the name of visitors of the poor, supported by their own ordinary callings, and never dreaming of being paid for their services".[31]

Arnold went on to develop an idea of ecumenical and sociological interest. "It does not seem improbable that many persons who now become preachers among the dissenters, without objecting to any of the doctrines of our Church, but simply because they have no means of following what they feel to be their calling in our communion, would gladly become deacons on the system suggested above, and would thus be useful to the Church instead of being in some sort opposed to it."[32] This he thought would be a step towards a comprehensive National Church and would distribute responsibility more widely within the Church, "giving all ranks of society their share in the administration of the Church".[33]

Arnold's deacons would be, in all spiritual functions, "under the direction and control of the presbyters of their respective parishes; but in temporal matters, such as the management and distribution of funds for charitable purposes, and in making provision for the bodily wants of the poor, they would form a council of which the presbyter would be the head, and to which all such matters might be entrusted".[34] Arnold envisaged no changes in the priesthood in function, training, or payment.

He proposed greater control over the preaching of deacons. "According to the present form of ordaining deacons, no deacon is authorised to preach, except he shall obtain the bishop's licence to do so. This provision might be enforced, and the licence to preach given only to such deacons as the bishop shall judge expedient, and might be granted only *durante bene placito*."[35] Arnold argued that by combining the relief of the poor with "the power of

[31] Ibid., p. 499.
[32] Ibid., p. 428.
[33] Ibid., p. 289; see also p. 119.
[34] Ibid., p. 427.
[35] Ibid., p. 428.

baptizing, of reading the Scriptures, and of preaching, when authorized by the bishop, deacons exhibited the peculiar character of Christianity, that of sanctifying the business of this world by doing everything in the name of the Lord Jesus".[36] They "would be expected to live in all things as became Christians, and the same standard would be followed by them which general opinion requires the clergy to conform to, but which it does not always enforce in the laity".[37]

Arnold held that the Canon Law made "a very wide distinction between the Deacon and the Presbyter; the Deacon, according to it, is half a layman and could return at any time to lay condition altogether; and I suppose no one is so mad as to maintain that a minister abstaining from all secular callings is a matter of necessity, seeing that St Paul carried on his trade of tentmaker even when he was an Apostle".[38] The Pluralities Act of 1838 forbade clergy to undertake secular work, with certain few exceptions; Arnold saw that it needed repeal before his scheme could take effect.

Since Arnold, a revived diaconate has had its advocates from the report of the Lower House of the Convocation of Canterbury on Home and Foreign Missions of 1857 to the report of the joint committee of the Convocation of Canterbury on the Revised Canon 83 of 1955. To-day those who wish to see an extension of the ordained ministry would scarcely be satisfied with a revived diaconate, while to many the development of the layman's rôle is a more pressing twentieth-century problem. To-day a more important sense of diaconate than that of an inferior order of clergy is increasingly occupying the mind of the Church—diaconate in the sense of the Church's ministry to the world in which all members of the Church share, but notably laymen in their secular occupations. Arnold's social thinking

[36] *Sermons, Christian Life,* etc., p. 415.

[37] *Miscellaneous Works,* p. 428.

[38] Stanley, p. 503.

included this sense of diaconate. He used his discussion about deacons to provoke imaginative thought on the Church's missionary problem in an industrial society. The particular problems to which Arnold proposed the solution of an extended order of deacons have largely disappeared. Laymen now have greater status in the Church and a larger part in its government. Recruitment to the ministry, although the number of ordained ministers may be inadequate, draws upon a wide social range. Lack of money and social status need prevent no man from entering the ordained ministry.

Arnold's Condemnation of the Oxford Movement

"No wise man doubts that the Reformation was imperfect or that in the Romish system there were many good institutions, and practices, and feelings, which it would be most desirable to restore amongst ourselves. Daily Church services, frequent communions, memorials of our Christian calling continually presented to our notice, in crosses and way-side oratories; commemorations of holy men, of all times and countries, the doctrine of the communion of saints practically taught; religious orders, especially of women, of different kinds, and under different rules, delivered only from the snare and sin of perpetual vows; all these, most of which are of some efficacy for good, even in a corrupt church, belong no less to the true Church and would there be purely beneficial."[39]

While Arnold was in sympathy with some aspects of the Oxford Movement he opposed many of its leading ideas, despite the fact that he had been a fellow of Oriel, and received spiritual guidance from John Keble. He composed no discourse of a systematic nature, but in the prefaces and appendices of his sermons, in his letters and other writings the undertones of criticism are present. The article which attracted most attention appeared unsigned in

[39] *Sermons,* 1849, Vol. IV, pp. lvi, ff.

the *Edinburgh Review* in April 1836 entitled "The Oxford Malignants".[40] It was a contribution to the controversy over the appointment of Dr Hampden[41] to the Regius Professorship of Divinity at Oxford in early 1836. In this essay, which Stanley did not see fit to reprint, Arnold attacked the Oxford Movement in language which critics have thought intemperate but which others have thought to be no harder than that used against the retiring but liberal Hampden.[42]

Keble had renounced Arnold's friendship when the latter published *Principles of Church Reform,* even though in earlier years it was Keble to whom Arnold turned for advice when he was in spiritual difficulties about ordination. In reply Arnold wrote a conciliatory letter in which, however, he held to his ground. Keble replied that the letter comforted him, but he trusted that Arnold could come nearer to Church views. "There was no getting on with Keble," said Tom Mozley, "without entire agreement, that is entire submission." J. A. Froude said: "If you did not agree with him there was something morally wrong with you."[43] When Pusey published his mighty tract on fasting, Arnold viewed it as antiquarian, and Hurrell Froude's *Remains* as impudent since they reviled "all those persons whom the accordant voice" of the Church of England, "without distinction of party, has agreed to honour, even perhaps with excess of admiration".[44]

[40] Op. cit., pp. 225-39. The title of the article was not of his choosing.

[41] Renn Dickson Hampden, 1793-1868; Bampton Lecturer, 1832; Principal of St Mary's Hall, Oxford, 1833; Professor of Moral Philosophy, 1834; Regius Professor of Divinity, 1836; Bishop of Hereford, 1847. Opposition to his election at Hereford occasioned Lord John Russell's reply to the Dean of Hereford: "Sir, I have the honour to receive your letter of the 23rd instant, in which you intimate to me your intention of violating the law."

[42] See G. Faber, *The Oxford Apostles,* London, Faber, 1933.

[43] Ibid., p. 89.

[44] Stanley, p. 484.

Arnold's article in the *Edinburgh Review* was the culmination of increasing differences of opinion and mutual criticism. In it he accused the adversaries of Hampden of garbling his writings in order to show up his supposed defects. "When men break through the charities and decencies of life to run down a good and pious individual", when they persecute, raising a cry which they know will arouse the worst passions and be re-echoed by baser followers, when they exploit party spirit, there is much of "mingled fraud, and baseness, and cruelty, of fanatical persecution".[45] Among conservatives at Oxford the appointment was regarded as another liberal blow against the Church. As something of a liberal or progressive himself Arnold may have under-estimated the emotion which coloured this reaction.

Reform was in the air and despite temporary obstructions it was to be successful. The Industrial Revolution had brought social change and a large scale increase and redistribution of population. Radical efforts were needed by the Church in this situation. To become self-conscious of the Church as a separate institution possessed of its own rights, privileges, and constitution—all held to be sacred—was not to be intellectually wrong, but, Arnold thought, morally powerless. To insist upon the Apostolic Succession, the episcopate as *de jure divino*, the Catholicity of the Church, and the nature of the priesthood in this revolutionary situation was both superstitious and irrevelant.

It was irrelevant to insist upon the Apostolic Succession, because it was a speculative belief engaging the attention of churchmen when they needed to bring themselves to practical action in the face of the profound social changes of the time and the power and influence of English Dissent. The Church, he thought, needed unity and efficiency not theological reappraisal. Yet there are times when an insti-

[45] This and the following quotations are from Arnold's *Edinburgh Review* article, unless it is otherwise stated.

tution must be thrown back upon itself, question its basic ideas and aims before it can satisfactorily come forward to inspire and lead as it should. When Arnold criticized the "Hophni and Phineas school" of "low worldly men . . . ministers not of the Gospel but of the aristocracy who belong to Christianity only from the accident of its being established by law" he was criticizing much of the immediate clerical vision and practice of the Church, which the new high churchmen revolted against as much as he did. In many ways Arnold's call was a prophetic one which died upon the ear. The Oxford men in the end emerged from their scholarship to be the leaders of a powerful movement which greatly affected the course of the Church's work. Arnold, of course, never lived to see it. But in the mid and late nineteenth century some of the men most devotedly working among the unskilled labouring poor of the new cities were high church clergymen.

Arnold's second objection was on theological grounds. It was superstitious to insist upon the Apostolic Succession. All that was associated with priestly power he disowned. A minister of the Gospel should be a teacher or governor or both; but to be a priest was "inconsistent with his office and cannot be assumed without profaneness".[46] It was wrong to think, as priesthood implied, that there was a perpetual supremacy of some men over others, and that their mediation was needed before acceptable worship could be offered to God. If "all men be of one race and of one intellectual and moral nature" the claim of superiority cannot stand. Arnold concedes the power of the Jewish priesthood but maintains they were counter-balanced by a succession of prophets, and they served also to be the type of the perfect priest who should come. Finally he claims that though we are dependent upon the Apostles' teaching for our religious knowledge, there is no evidence that they

[46] *Sermons, Christian Life and Doctrine*, ed. Forster, London, 1878, appendix to Sermon XI, p. 269.

claimed priestly powers, nor that their successors possessed any extraordinary powers.

Some practical points follow. "It is one thing to ordain that in the public and common service of the Church prayers should be offered, and the sacraments administered, only by those whose particular business it is to minister in the congregation; and another to assert, that essentially, and not as a matter of order, but really and spiritually there can be no true sacramental commemoration of Christ's death without the presence of a minister." For the latter there is no New Testament warrant.

The power of the keys is no support for priestly ideas. If by this idea is meant "a real power to forgive or refuse forgiveness spiritually to the souls of sinners so that he on whom the minister pronounces absolution becomes thereby cleared of sin in the sight of God and he to whom he refuses it remains unforgiven by God", this is unchristian and unscriptural. To Arnold the power of the keys was the power to exercise Church discipline. But this could be exercised by any to whom the Church had committed authority; and it also transferred the question from doctrine to government. What then did the minister have? The "ordinary power of teaching and government, with such peculiarities in addition as arise from the peculiar character and sanctions with which the doctrine taught us was originally invested; that is when we proclaim the Gospel promises and the Gospel principles of life; the divine sanction originally given to them accompanies in like manner our delivery of them".

The ministry in fact possesses "great moral power derived from apostolical teaching through Scriptures" and this quite independent of any "pretended Apostolical Succession". Moreover, episcopacy could not be maintained *de jure divino*. "As the abstract Church or Christian society is divided into a great number of particular churches, each having its own laws, in all matters not already provided for by the common divine law of the Scriptures, so each Church may appoint its own ministers, whether teachers or governors, in such a manner and with powers as it shall judge convenient. And all ministers so appointed, under whatever different title, and with whatever different powers if they teach the same Gospel, which the Apostles taught, and govern people after the principle of Christ's law—they are the true and only successors of the Apostles."

He concludes that the ministry decided nothing about the nature of Church government positively, but it does overthrow the claim of any one form to be received as by divine commandment.

A great danger which Arnold saw in the doctrines of the Oxford men was the creation of a wedge between two parts of the Church. In his view, to distinguish between the clergy and the laity, as these doctrines must, prevents the real triumph of the Gospel. A distinction comes to be drawn between the Church (the clergy) and the Faithful (the laity). There is also a mischievous separation of spiritual and temporal powers. The Henrican reformation united both the temporal and spiritual in the lawful head of a Christian commonwealth. Subsequent events resulted in a further separation, while the distinction between Church and State even in a Christian country also grew. All these are the regrettable consequences of a wrong-headed doctrine, from whose grips the Church of England had broken free. The opinions which Arnold opposed were precisely those which the Oxford Movement magnified to the destruction of a true notion of the Church and its ministry and in particular they prevented, in Arnold's view, the development of a comprehensive National Church.

In addition to these theological and political difficulties there was a difference of scholastic temperament between Arnold and the Oxford men. He had a better grasp of history than they. Under the influence, perhaps, of the Romantic Revival they tended to take an idealized view of the Middle Ages, which Arnold was not able to do. He was more concerned with Scripture than with traditions and this with his historical sense gave him greater ability to deal with critical questions in a less conservative way. Both Rose and Pusey were conversant with the works of German critical scholarship and both reacted against them. Arnold, on the other hand, recommended Vaughan to master German in order to read the German theologians, whose writings "seem to me to be a most pure transcript of the New Testament, combining in a most extraordinary degree the spirit of wisdom."[47]

It is perhaps significant that the Oxford Movement produced devoted priests and Arnold's school dedicated laymen in responsible positions in public life.

[47] Stanley, p. 352. In classical studies Arnold had the friendship of Bunsen (see p. 29), who was secretary to the great historian, Barthold Georg Niebuhr (1776-1831), while Niebuhr was Prussian ambassador in Rome. Niebuhr retired to Bonn in 1823, where Arnold visited him. "He was haunted by history", Lionel Trilling on Thomas Arnold in *Matthew Arnold,* p. 45.

5

PRINCIPLES OF CHURCH REFORM

THE religious and political situation in the 1820's and 1830's to Arnold, as to many other shrewd observers, was dire. Stanley writes: "The disturbances of the time . . . struck on some of the most sensitive of his natural feelings —his sense of justice, and his impatience of the sight of suffering; they seemed to him symptoms of a deep-seated disease in all the relations of English society—the results of a long series of evils from the neglect of the eighteenth century—of the lawlessness of the feudal system—of the oppressions of the Norman Conquest—of the dissoluteness of the Roman Empire—of the growth of those social and national sins which the Hebrew prophets had denounced, and which Chrisitianity in its full practical development was designed to check."[1] The law of moral consequences in history was working itself out and to Arnold's mind he and his contemporaries of the early nineteenth century had to pay the penalty for the sins of the past as well as for their own. To the *Sheffield Courant* in 1831 he wrote of the Church's responsibilities in the new industrial areas: "It is not too late now—but in five years it will be."[2] There is an urgency about Arnold's writings on reform.

As a true disciple of S. T. Coleridge, Arnold was strongly in favour of Establishment. "My conviction of the benefits of a Church Establishment arises from this: that thus and thus only, can we ensure the dispersion of a number of

[1] Op. cit., p. 242.

[2] *Miscellaneous Works,* p. 211.

well-educated men over the whole kingdom, whose sole business it is, *to do good of the highest kind,* to enforce, in their public teaching, the purest principles and practice that mankind have ever yet been made acquainted with; and to exhibit these in their own persons in all their daily intercourse with their neighbours, instructing the young, visiting the sick, relieving, advising and maintaining the cause of the poor: and spreading amongst all ranks the wholesome influence of a good life, a cultivated understanding, and the feelings and manners of a true gentleman."[3]

Arnold was not convinced that the clergy were in fact adequately equipped for this task. Their understanding of contemporary society and its problems he felt was limited and their grasp of history weak. Arnold's pamphlet in support of the repeal of the Test Act and of the emancipation of Roman Catholics[4] raised the issue of the clergy's competence to decide historical questions since they made little attempt to study history.

On the basis of a good Biblical and theological education Arnold wished to see an improvement in the clergy's understanding of contemporary society. In the introduction to one of his volumes of sermons he wrote:

"The minister is destined to lead a life eminently active, to be thrown amongst his brethren without any more particular occupation than that of promoting their good in every way temporal and spiritual. It is manifest, therefore, that he ought fully to understand the nature of that society which he is to endeavour to influence; the relations of its several parts to one another; what may have disordered those relations; the views which the several classes entertain of each other and of themselves; and how far these are founded on prejudice or on truth. . . . The existence of religious dissent, combined as it often is with political party

[3] *Miscellaneous Works,* pp. 219-20.

[4] *The Christian Duty of Conceding the Claims of the Roman Catholics, Miscellaneous Works,* pp. 1-78.

feelings, makes it fitting that he should well understand the history of his own country, in the true sense of the term. This knowledge is not to be gained by reading what is called ecclesiastical history only; for works of this sort, even when they are not the mere statement of one sect or faction, are yet too limited in their range to give a comprehensive view of the whole subject; but by reading ecclesiastical and civil history together, and by so endeavouring to obtain a clear knowledge of the several parties and sects in their complex character, part political and part religious, and to understand which of these two elements has predominated, and how it has acted upon the other." The parties of England, for example, he considered to follow those divisions which had agitated mankind since the first beginnings of political society. "Here is the enduring value of the great philosophers of Greece and Rome; that with a perfect abstraction from those particular names and association which are for ever biassing our judgement in modern and domestic instances, the great principles of all political questions . . . are perfectly discussed." Arnold concluded: "I would have him (the minister) turn to a definite account knowledge which he now picks up carelessly and often leaves undigested: I would have him master of those subjects upon which all not only talk but act, and on which it is to be desired that some at least should be able to talk and act sensibly."[5] Only by such a contemporary training would the Church be able to come to grips with contemporary problems, from which the clergy, for the most part, were debarred from contributing constructively by their lack of training.

It is interesting to note that Arnold was an advocate of careful social analysis, which beginning in his time, became the basis for much practical reform, and which is now an accepted tool of administration. He wrote, for example, of the need to "collect facts relative to the condi-

[5] *Christian Life and Doctrine,* p. ix, f.

tion of the labouring classes and to bring them to the knowledge of the public", and he listed the heads of such an inquiry: analysis of population, wages, places of birth, and origins of the labouring population, religious affiliations, schools, housing, food, literature read, and, where possible, indications of trends.[6] He made some effort to promote a society which would collect information on these matters but apparently it came to nothing.

Arnold's pamphlet on Church reform was an outstanding contribution though controversial and widely misunderstood, among many contributions to a great discussion of reform in all aspects of the nation.[7] In later years Arnold withdrew from some of his more extreme positions and stressed the sense of urgency with which he set down his proposals in 1833.

[6] *Miscellaneous Works,* pp. 483-4, and Bamford, *Thomas Arnold,* pp. 204-5.

[7] It was widely read. Four editions appeared in six months. *The Times* gave it a lengthy review on 25 and 26 January 1833. It stirred some violent reactions. Keble's has been already mentioned but Stanley records others (Ch. VII). Gloyn writes: "Following publication of the pamphlet Church newspapers attacked him, he was denounced almost by name in the University pulpit at Oxford . . . the general sale of his Sermons was almost stopped . . . his personal acquaintances began to look upon him with alarm." (Stanley, pp. 290-1.) Even such Liberal churchmen as Whately and Hawkins disapproved, Hawkins implying that Arnold was writing on subjects he did not understand and which were not within his proper province (cf. Arnold's letters to Hawkins, Stanley, pp. 301-4). Arnold was grieved that so many of his friends regarded his pamphlet as latitudinarian in point of doctrine. But their lack of understanding or sympathy made him more determined to examine and develop his principles (p. 94).

There were written replies. The chaplain to the Archbishop of Dublin, C. Dickinson, see p. 171, "a person of junior standing" to Arnold as Stanley remarks, wrote a reply, *Observations on Ecclesiastical Legislature and Church Reform,* which drew from Arnold a postscript, added to the 4th edition. From Oxford, William Palmer replied with *Remarks on the Rev. Dr Arnold's Principles of Church Reform,* 1833. There was also L. Carpenter's *Brief Notes on the Rev. Dr Arnold's Principles of Church Reform,* 1833.

The 1820's witnessed the gathering momentum of reform. A number of efforts had been made to equalize incomes amongst the clergy, some progress towards the removal of the disabilities of the Roman Catholics had been in the air for a time, but had been so far frustrated by the monarch. At last in 1828 the Test Act was removed, and full emancipation came in 1829. In support of this Arnold had composed his pamphlet, *The Christian Duty of Conceding the Claims of the Roman Catholics,* which, as Stanley states, created an unfavourable body of clerical opinion against Arnold. The pamphlet is noteworthy, however, for its conception of the connection between religion and politics, containing as it does some of Arnold's most concise views on political philosophy. In 1833 the suppression of a number of Irish bishoprics was under debate, while at the same time the Dissenters were pressing for a reform of the Established Church of England and the consequent acceptance of the voluntary principle for religious bodies, as already operated amongst the Nonconformists themselves. When many of the clergy appealed in the courts against the loss of the full value of their tithes the dissenting protests became a raging torrent. "The Established Church is a great national evil . . . it is an obstacle to the progress of truth and godliness in the land . . . therefore its end is most devoutly to be wished by every lover of God and man",[8] so a leading Congregationalist wrote. Petition after petition rolled into Parliament beseeching the Members that Dissenters should not be obliged to contribute to Anglican worship, and that further the State should be regarded as secular and neutral towards all creeds. This was a view with which Arnold's whole thinking disagreed, but one which appeared to have a reasonable chance of success. The Dissenters numbered two million out of a population of ten million in 1815 and in the north of England they may well have been in the majority.

[8] Halévy, *A History of the English People,* Vol. 3.

Even in 1815 they possessed more places of worship than the Church of England. Such numerical pressure, especially when it began to be allied with Radical politicians, appeared to be overwhelming. When Arnold uttered his famous aphorism, "The Church, as it now stands, no human power can save",[9] he spoke not only with reference to the Church's spiritual state, but also with an eye to the very heavy criticism to which the National Church was subjected. "My pamphlet", he wrote, "was written on the supposition—not implied but expressed repeatedly—that the Church Establishment was in extreme danger; and therefore I proposed remedies, which although I do still sincerely believe them to be in themselves right and good, yet would be manifestly chimerical and to advise them might well be called indiscreet, had not the danger alarms, as I supposed, been imminent."[10]

What finally drove Arnold into print was a pamphlet of Lord Henley's.[11] This was the most influential of all pamphlets published on Church reform. He argued the need to increase the number of bishoprics, to reform the incongruities of the ecclesiastical system, and also that parliament was obliged to advance as much as would maintain a resident minister in every parish, and would support a parochial minister in towns for every four thousand souls. Lord Henley argued that the State had no right to confiscate the Church's endowments, which had been donated in order that the Church perform its spiritual functions. But the question must be asked: Was the Church carrying out the donors' intentions? The State could interfere to ensure that the Church had regard to them, and if necessary it could alter the contract so as to answer the purpose for which the donation was granted to the Church. The

[9] Stanley, p. 278. [10] Ibid., p. 287.

[11] *A Plan for Church Reform,* 1832. Robert Henley Eden, 2nd Baron Henley, 1789-1841; Master in Chancery, 1826; greatly interested in Church reform and published pamphlets on the subject.

Church was regarded, in the widest sense, as a Corporation, and thus the State could redistribute the endowments to make the Church's task of evangelization more effective. In other words, there should be a redistribution of Church properties and moneys, and even Disestablishment, in order that Church endowments might be properly used. Henley himself thought that the Establishment should be ended by reason of ecclesiastical failure and a voluntary principle of churches accepted, which would, of course, in Arnold's view, undermine the whole basic constitution of the Church of England in the life of the nation. He wrote to Whately: "My reasons for writing it (the pamphlet) were chiefly because the reform proposed by Lord Henley and others seemed to me not only insufficient, but of a wrong kind; and because I have heard the American doctrine of every man paying his minister as he would his lawyer advanced and supported in high quarters, where it sounded alarming. I was also struck by the great vehemence displayed by the Dissenters at the late elections, and by the refusal to pay Church-rates at Birmingham. Nothing, as it seems to me can save the Church, but a union with the Dissenters; now they are leagued with the antichristian party, and no merely internal reforms in the administration of the actual system will, I think, or can satisfy them."[12]

The technical preservation of the Establishment, however, was assured when it was perceived that the agitation was noisier in the land than it was influential in Parliament; though the Dissenters in the course of time came to win substantial financial concessions. The Church was able to muster considerable support as a number of addresses to the Archbishop of Canterbury displayed. At the same time the Liberals began to discover something of the usefulness of being able to create their own bishops.

Arnold himself was pessimistic about the possibility of

[12] Stanley, pp. 297-8.

many of his hopes being realized, although in the course of time a number of them were, but he never abandoned his conviction of the pressing need for Church reform. Shortly before his death he wrote to Archdeacon Hare: "I feel so deeply the danger and evil of the false Church system, that despairing of seeing the true Church restored I am disposed to cling, not from choice, but necessity, to the Protestant tendency of laying the whole stress on Christian religion, and adjourning the notion of Church *sine die*."[13] Stanley records this mark of Arnold's in 1839: "When I think of the Church I could sit down and pine and die." Stanley continues: "And it is remarkable to observe the joyous tone of his sermons on Easter Day, as the birthday of Christ's Religion, and the tone of subdued and earnest regret which marks those on Whit Sunday, as the birthday of the Christian Church: 'Easter Day we keep as the birthday of a living friend; Whit Sunday we keep as the birthday of a dead friend'."[14]

The pamphlet on Church reform is a discussion of principles. The practical conclusions for reform derive from the principles. Arnold wrote to the *Sheffield Courant*: "I most earnestly admire and love a Church Establishment; and because it has in it the means of doing all this (i.e. civilizing the nation), better, I think than any other sect of Christians, therefore I value and would most rigorously reform *the actual* Church Establishment."[15] A comprehensive National Church could only be achieved by reform. "I have nothing to dread from reform. On the contrary, as an enemy of revolution, I have everything to hope from it. I wish it to be deep, searching and universal: I wish it to extend to church and state, to army, navy, law, trade and education; to our political and social institutions; to our

[13] Ibid., pp. 637-8. Julius Charles Hare, 1795-1855; Fellow of Trinity Coll., Camb., 1818; Rector of Herstmonceux, 1832; Archdeacon of Lewes, 1840.

[14] Ibid., p. 492.

[15] *Miscellaneous Works,* p. 220.

habits, principles, and practice, both as citizens and men. God grant that reform may so have its perfect work as equally to crush and bring to nothing the conservatives and the Jacobins, those equal enemies of all good, whose alternating crimes and follies have, between them, been the curse of mankind from the very beginning of history."[16]

The basic principle is that of a comprehensive National Church, embracing all denominations and all members of the English nation. A contributor to *A History of the Ecumenical Movement* remarks that Arnold "put forward the most definite, perhaps the only definite, scheme for home reunion that appeared during the nineteenth century."[17]

Arnold argued first of all that the structure of the Church should be adapted to the new industrial society of the early nineteenth century. In a letter to the *Sheffield Courant* he listed those structural reforms, many of which in fact took place in subsequent years as a result of Government inquiry and pressure and as a result of general pressure within and without the Church. (We may illustrate Arnold's ideas on reform from other writings than *Principles of Church Reform*, the text of which follows, since in that pamphlet he sets down systematically what he advocates in many other places.)

"1st. A Commutation of tithes, even if it can only be effected at a great loss to the Church, because it is far better that the Church should be somewhat poorer, if at such a price it can remove what is at present a great cause of offence.

"2nd. An entire remodelling of the Episcopal Order, that many scandals may be removed, and the Church obtain an efficient government. For this object it seems essential:

1st. That Translations should be made illegal.

[16] Ibid., p. 236.

[17] Op. cit., ed. R. Rouse and S. C. Neill, London, S.P.C.K., 1954, p. 274.

2nd. That the incomes of the small Bishoprics be increased out of the larger ones, as to supersede the necessity of annexing to them Deaneries, livings held in commendam, or any other ecclesiastical preferment whatsoever.

"3rd. That the Dioceses be divided, so as to give the Church an efficient government. For this purpose all Deaneries should be made Bishoprics, retaining their present incomes, and of course with no seats in Parliament. The Prebends should be annexed to underpaid livings in large towns, and the largest Church in all such towns should be erected into a Bishop's See; so that there should be no great towns throughout England without its resident Bishop, who without being raised to any undue elevation in rank and fortune, would yet in both be sufficiently respectable to maintain the just influence of the Church with the higher classes as well as with the poor.

"4th. That in all large towns and populous districts a sufficient number of new parishes be created, with a resident minister to each. Funds might be provided by annexing, for the future, every one of those new parishes to some valuable country living, if possible in the same neighbourhood or county. Any incumbent accepting such living for the time to come being bound to reside in his town parish nine months in the year, and to keep a resident curate on his benefice in the country.

"5th. The Church government being thus rendered efficient, by reducing the size of the dioceses to what would be within the power of an individual to manage, a system of ecclesiastical jurisdiction should be framed, for the prompt punishment, not only of scandalous vice in the clergy—which is, happily, very rare—but of what may be called unclerical conduct and neglect of duty; so that the class of "sporting clergy", as they are called, should be gradually weeded out of the establishment.

"These reforms would, I am persuaded, work a change in the usefulness of the Church, and in the state of feeling towards it, especially in the manufacturing districts, which would be well worth purchasing at the cost of far greater innovations."[18]

Arnold then argued that Dissenters should be comprehended in the National Church on the basis of union in a common task, not of uniformity of belief. Again to the *Sheffield Courant* he wrote: "I see then some cause of Dissent existing which a needful reform in our own Establishment would remove; others again are independent of any conceivable extent of reform; while a third class are indeed invincible obstacles to *uniformity*, but ought to be none to union. And he who knows the history of the Christian Church has too good cause to remember how fatally the pursuit of this foolish phantom uniformity has lured men from the attainment of the real and substantial blessing, union."[19] This passage reveals the temper of mind with which Arnold approached the Dissenters and their comprehension within the National Church. For him unity is the product of common obedience in a cause rather than the product of uniformity of belief. He continually returns to this point, which plays an important part in his thinking about Church and State. "All societies of men, whether we call them states or churches, should make their bond to consist in a common object and a common practice, rather than in a common belief; in other words, their end should be good rather than truth. We may consent to act together, but we cannot consent to believe together; many motives may persuade us to the one; we may like the object, or we may like the company, or we may think it safest to join them, or most convenient, and any one of these motives is quite sufficient to induce a unity of action, action being a thing in our own power. But no motives can persuade us to believe together; we may wish a statement to be true, we may admire those

[18] *Miscellaneous Works,* pp. 220-1. [19] Ibid., p. 225.

who believe it, we may find it very inconvenient not to believe it; all this helps us nothing; unless our own mind is freely convinced that the statement of doctrine be true, we cannot by possibility believe it. That union in action will in the end lead very often to union of belief is most true; but we cannot ensure its doing so; and the social bond cannot directly require for its perfectness more than union of action. It cannot properly require more than it is in the power of men to give; and men can submit their actions to a common law at their own choice, but their internal conviction they cannot. Such a union of action appears historically to have been the original bond of the Christian Church."[20]

In *Principles of Church Reform,* Arnold does discuss the question of doctrinal differences and concludes that in the case of the major dissenting bodies separation is not the result of doctrinal differences but of non-theological factors and that the issue of belief, therefore, does not stand in the way of comprehension. Previous attempts to form a comprehensive National Church had collapsed in the face of doctrinal tests. Arnold, however, rightly saw that underneath disputes about doctrine and liturgy lay a substantial area of practical as well as dogmatic agreement, which centred on the moral precepts of the Gospel, the doctrine of the Trinity and the uniqueness of the saving work of Christ. Roman Catholics, because of their allegiance to Rome, and Unitarians, because of their denial of the divinity of Christ, presented difficulties. Arnold thought they could be overcome. He made bold to suggest that a National Church of England should propose no tests in doctrine but allow variety of opinion. Since, he considered, it was foolish to think that all men, at all times, and in all places would think alike, it was unrealistic to attempt to recreate a unified Church upon a detailed doctrinal basis. Moreover, he

[20] *Introductory Lectures on Modern History,* Oxford, 1842, pp. 50-1.

held that not only variety of opinion but variety of practice should be allowed. All that should be required was acceptance of a common faith in God and our Saviour.

This aspect of the pamphlet provoked a great storm of theological, historical, and personal criticism. The very idea of refusing to make detailed doctrinal tests was obnoxious to those who regarded them as bulwarks of the Church in the traditional social order. To others it was the abandonment of all that they held dear in their conception of the Church and its essential unity. To-day no serious discussion between Churches of doctrinal differences would start from such a liberal, and indeed cavalier, disregard for the issues of truth in Christian doctrine. Even if the Ecumenical Movement has discovered non-theological factors in disunity, it has not taught its adherents to abandon truth as they see it. Of Arnold's argument it can be said that such tests of doctrine have been a constant cause of division in the Church at all times, and specially since the Reformation; and in reality some accommodation has to be made between primary and secondary points of doctrine. Arnold never thought, as some critics implied, that the scheme was immediately practicable. His aim was to force the Church to recognize the gravity of the situation and encourage it to act bravely in it, by seeking some "rapprochement" with the Dissenters who were strong enough to turn the scale either for or against an Establishment; more especially because they were in league with the Radicals to bring the Establishment down and would destroy it utterly if they were not taken into the camp in the defence of it.

The old Hookerian ideal was a possible way out, if modified in the light of the need to make some real concession to the very powerful Nonconformist element in English life. It has been urged by Dr S. C. Carpenter that Arnold despised the only real instrument, the Church of England, which he possessed to Christianize the nation.[21] But criticism does not mean disloyalty or lack of affection. Stanley writes: "His love of reform was in exact proportion to his love of the institution which he wished to reform." He quotes Archdeacon Hare as saying that Arnold was restless of evils which were capable of remedy.[22]

[21] S. C. Carpenter, *Church and People, 1789-1889*, S.P.C.K., 1933, p. 60 f.

[22] Stanley, p. 176.

6

ARNOLD'S SIGNIFICANCE TO-DAY

To read Arnold is to acquire a healthy perspective upon the Church history of the nineteenth century.[1] It is to be confronted by searching questions about the Church's mission in an industrial society, now becoming worldwide. Arnold is significant as a missionary theologian. His significance does not lie in his detailed proposals of reform. He himself was aware that particular reforms did not go to the root of the Church's missionary problem and in giving his pamphlet the title *Principles of Church Reform* showed that his thinking went beyond particular items of reform, even if in the popular mind of the Church he was identified with some of his more unconventional suggestions.

Much that Arnold proposed has come into effect in the century since he wrote. The agitation for reform in Church and State in the 1830's led to a considerable overhaul of the Church's machinery. Peel's Commission and the Ecclesi-

[1] "Much excellent work has been done on the Puritans of the middle of the 17th century, but far too little on the Dissenters of the 18th. . . . Much has been done on the Wesleys and their immediate followers, but far too little on the wider aspects of the great evangelical revival. The problem of the relation of Church and State in England seems to have excited less interest among historians the nearer they got to the year 1900. . . . Even more urgent is the need for a general historical work on Church and State covering the whole of the 19th century in England. However, very much of the religious history of the 19th century would repay the attention it might receive if only historians would resist the temptation to write more books on the early years of the Oxford Movement." G. K. Clark, *The English Inheritance,* S.C.M., 1950, p. 11.

astical Commissioners devised juster distribution of income and property within the Church. Church extension went ahead with the creation of new dioceses in industrial areas, the creation of new parishes, and the building of new churches in the rapidly growing cities. More trouble was taken with the training of clergy; theological colleges were being founded before Arnold's death. Laymen gradually came to have more say in the government of the Church, and the Enabling Act of 1919 set up a system of Parochial Church Councils, Diocesan Conferences, and a National Assembly of the Church, in which at all three levels, laymen have a place. Furthermore, the last fifty years have seen a "rapprochement" between the Church of England and the Free Churches. Collaboration through Councils of Churches and official conversations and negotiations between the Churches is the expression of a very different spirit than that of the nineteenth-century controversies over education or church rates. Even if the increasingly minority position in which all the Churches, but especially the Free Churches, find themselves, has contributed to this "rapprochement", it represents an advance towards that comprehensive National Church which Arnold desired.

The words of a recent historian sum up the position: "As time passed, many of the ideals of Arnold came to be quietly adopted in the Church, though not yet in their fullness or in every detail; Arnold and Stanley would have felt themselves quite at home as members of the joint gathering of Anglicans and Free Churchmen which in 1950 produced the report *Church Relations in England*."[2] Yet if Arnold's contribution to the Church, as a theologian and social commentator, were to be reduced to certain measures of reform, most of which gradually were put into effect, then any study of Arnold would be an antiquarian attempt to trace the outlines of battles long forgotten and little in-

[2] Stephen Neill, *Anglicanism,* Pelican Books, 1958, p. 247.

telligible to the present. Arnold could be dismissed as one of the many stimulators of reform with a vision somewhat ahead of his time.

Arnold's contribution is on a deeper level than that of reform. Yet even on that level the reforms of the last century leave the Church of England far from being the comprehensive National Church which he thought the Established Church should be. To-day, even if all that Arnold advocated had been put into effect, deeper problems of mission in the culture of an industrial society would remain. Arnold's significance lies in his perspectives, in his view of the rôle of the Church in the world, and particularly in the presuppositions upon which this view rested. It is a significance independent of the limitations which his own time and situation imposed upon him.

Arnold writes, although with a keen eye and ear for the important social event, away from the main stream of political and industrial life. In more than one passage of his correspondence he regrets this fact. In addition, he belongs to the generation preceding the great critical and scientific controversies which stirred the mid nineteenth century. His son, Matthew, typified the adventurous Christian mind wrestling with the new intellectual problems on the frontiers of theology, science, and philosophy. Certainly Arnold's attraction to German biblical criticism shows where he might have stood in the later critical debates, but Matthew is a modern religious man in a sense in which his father is not. Arnold's writings, and notably the moving private diary of the last months of his life, from which Stanley takes many extracts for his chapter on Arnold's last days and death, express a direct and confident trust in a view of the world which was no longer possible to many Christian minds in his son's day, nor ours. Between the generations there is a watershed. Thomas Arnold is in the ancient world of Christian belief; Matthew Arnold, who hears the "melancholy, long, withdrawing roar" of "the Sea of Faith", is in the modern world of Christian belief.

On the other hand Arnold wrote within the context of industrial society. Industry and society have changed in many ways since the 1830's, but the outlines of the Church's missionary problem in an industrial society were there then and Arnold saw them. Then the situation was more fluid; it took considerable understanding to grasp the essentials of it. To-day the problem has taken on a greater intensity, as industrial society has in the past century developed its own culture with its characteristic ways of thinking based mainly on the positive sciences. To-day the Christian mission faces a much graver intellectual task than in Arnold's time, but his perspectives set him in the right way to understand the missionary problem of the Church in an industrial society.

The first perspective of Arnold's thinking was sociological. He had a clear understanding of the social context in which the Church was placed after the Industrial Revolution, and saw that any effective strategy of mission must be based on such an understanding. This is a lesson not yet learned by the Church, but one which, taken seriously, would lead to radical changes in policy and structure. Perhaps Arnold's own understanding of the social context contained a stronger element of compassion than of rational analysis, yet this would be most natural in a man of strong Christian conviction in the crude and often vicious world of early industrialism. Arnold's portraits of the condition of the working class are often no less agonizing than Engels'[3] or, later, Taine's in his *Notes on England*.[4]

Arnold saw that there were social pressures upon men

[3] F. Engels, *The Condition of the Working Class in England in 1844*.

[4] There is a recent English translation by Edward Hyams, Thames and Hudson, 1957. Taine paid a long visit to England in 1859, and shorter ones in 1862 and 1871.

which affected their religious attitudes and behaviour. In the crude conflict of the factory system and in the miserable "East Ends" of industrial cities, apart from the Church's failure to provide adequate facilities for religious practice, Christian faith was at a discount. The new populations coming into the cities to work in the factories came from a countryside which was still largely practising; their religious habits and attitudes could not be transplanted into the new industrial, urban situation. There had to be a new expression of Christianity, a new set of structures. The Church's programme of building, of drawing new parish boundaries, of appointments of ministers, was in most areas in the nineteenth century too little, too late, and too conservative. Arnold wrote at a time when this failure of the Church to react adequately to the new situation was becoming apparent to the keen eye. He saw the situation, he saw the need and felt a great sense of urgency.

Although the techniques and disciplines of sociology and its near relation, psychology, were then in a primitive state, Arnold does in fact look at the Church's problem in the society of his day through the eyes of a sociologist and psychologist. To do this in the 1830's was a great achievement. His contemporaries abstracted religion from its social context. The Evangelical fostered a personal religion; the Tractarians isolated and idealized the Church. This process of abstraction led Arnold to condemn many aspects of the religion of his time. He thought, for example, that in their discussions the Tractarians were turning the doctrine of apostolic succession into "a profane, heraldic theory".

In so far as the Church is a temporal institution and subject to the same sociological forces as other institutions, the eye of the sociologist may fall on the Church as well as on the society in which it is set. Such sociological studies of the Church itself are useful instruments for the Church's policymakers. Arnold's sociological perspective included this kind of examination of the Church. To-day, with the improvement of sociological studies, the possibilities of such examination are much greater. Most Churches have developed machinery for collecting statistics of membership and practice; they can thus assess their general standing in society. Some Churches, notably the Roman Catholic Church in France,[5] have through systematic and often detailed surveys isolated particular problems, such as certain age groups, or certain occupations and social groups, or certain regions. Only in rare cases have sociological studies of religion probed in depth into religious attitudes and culture and their relations with society as a whole. Such studies in depth, putting flesh and blood on the bare bones of statistics and containing where possible a historical point of view, are the next stage. They are attempts to find answers to the problems posed by statistics and the large scale surveys. The intelligent use of the conclusions of such studies will depend on the policy of a particular Church. If such studies give accurate pictures of the Church in its situation in modern industrialized and largely dechristianized society, they are likely to point to radical policy de-

[5] A general account of this work in France is to be found in Canon F. Boulard's *Introduction to Religious Sociology,* Trsl. M. J. Jackson, Darton, Longman and Todd, 1960, and more briefly in *La Sociologie Religieuse,* Editions Spes, 1957 (a special number of "Cahiers d'Action Religieuse et Sociale" produced by the organization, Action Populaire). Examples of this work are the report of the diocesan census in Marseilles in 1953—Mgr Gros, *La Pratique Religieuse dans le Diocèse de Marseille,* Paris, Editions Ouvrières, 1954; a model study in depth of a parish (St Pothin at Lyons), E. Pin, *Pratique Religieuse et Classes Sociales,* Paris, Editions Spes, 1956; among urban studies there is *Grenoble, Essai de Sociologie Religieuse,* 1953, by Mme Jean Perrot from the Centre D'Etudes des Complexes Sociales, 2 rue Jean-Macé, Grenoble, and among rural studies the analysis of the diocese of Séez in Normandy, *Pratique Religieuse et Orientations Pastorales,* 1956, from Direction des Oeuvres, Alençon, Orne, both of which relate religious practice to the social, political, and economic situations and problems of the areas in question.

cisions. There is always a danger, however, because of the conservative nature of the Church as an institution, that the conclusions of sociological studies might be used for the redeployment of resources within or the improvement of existing structure and machinery, rather than for a radical policy of mission. Arnold's sociological thinking in the 1830's led him to such a radical policy of mission.

Arnold's other main perspective was theological. It is difficult to separate the two; a sociological perspective derives from theological presuppositions about the purpose and rôle of the Church in society. The use made of the conclusions of sociological studies depends on a Church's theological understanding of itself. In his thinking about the rôle of the Church in society, Arnold is a teacher for us to-day.

Arnold saw that the Church should have a positive concern for society. His vision of a National Church, in the great tradition of Hooker in which Church and State are religious and political aspects of the same society, may well have been far from the reality of nineteenth-century England as it is to-day, but it expresses an important criterion for judging the Church's relations with society. The Church for Arnold had the duty of Christianizing not only the individuals but also the institutions of society. Christian, biblical principles should be the basis and conscience of institutions, which have such formative power over the thinking and behaviour of those people involved in them—an important sociological insight of Arnold's. His interest in the reform of many institutions of his day—national and local government, industry, education, University, and Church—is an attempt to approximate these institutions to Christian principles.

Holding this position Arnold saw much to criticize in the Church. In the first place he deplored that the Church and its ministry should preach a private morality in the face of the many social evils of the day. He understood well that social morality dictated private morality. The insight was not shared by the majority of the clergy, notably the Evangelicals, who reduced their social concern to occasional descents into the wider field to protest and fight against some glaring social evil. This is not uncommon to-day, but to Arnold the Christian concern with society was a continuing involvement, an attempt to infect and infuse society and its institutions with the Christian conscience. The frontier idea of to-day is in the Arnold tradition. With a better understanding of itself as the laity in the world, dispersed in the various sectors of life, the Church is moving nearer to Arnold's position.

In the second place Arnold criticized those sections of the Church which fell into the temptation to reflect the conventional morality and ideology of the nation or of a section of the nation, notably the middle classes, since then as now the structure of the Church of England was far from an exact parallel of the structure of the nation. This temptation to reflect conventional morality and ideology is peculiarly one of an Established Church with close links at its head with political government and with a large amount of lay patronage. At a time of rapid social change and of considerable social distress for the Church to fall into this temptation was to side with the conservative and oppressive forces in society. The victims of the new social order could see the Church only as a conservative institution condoning injustice. Much of the great Marxist onslaught on religion rests on evidence collected by Marx and Engels in this country, where they found the Churches to reflect the conventional morality of the time and to give a religious tinge to it. In order to draw the Church from this unhappy position, although in this endeavour subsequent history shows that he had little success, Arnold urged a continuing social concern and involvement, and also flexibility, so that the Church should be able to devise new structures to meet new situations and so that it should be in a position to pass effective judgement on its own rôle in society. Arnold disliked the endorsement of conventional morality because by its nature it was uncritical.

Arnold's third criticism was of that section of the Church of England and of other Churches which were sectarian in tendency. The continuing social concern meant involvement, no distinction between sacred and secular, a rôle for the ministry of Christianizing the national lite at all levels. In Arnold's time some of the best minds of the Church, in particular the Oxford men, were thinking in terms of detachment from the world and abstraction into a religious preserve, in their view, in the best interests of the Church. They shared Arnold's view about the Church's self-criticism but not his view of the involvement of the Church with society. Thus Arnold condemned the Oxford Movement as sectarian. His slashing attack in the *Edinburgh Review* is said to have helped greatly to arouse that suspicion in the minds of average Englishmen towards Anglo-Catholics which they have never lost. In his condemnation of sectarian tendencies Arnold was not able to see the positive contribution which the Oxford Movement could make to the Church. In fact the survival of the Church of England itself in some form, then in question, may well have rested on a certain detachment, a retrenchment, and a new consciousness of the Church as the Church in its distinction from society. Furthermore, the Oxford Movement sent a number of able and heroic clergy into some of the worst industrial areas and later in the nineteenth century played a part in a revival of the Church's social concern. This was not apparent in the beginnings of the Oxford Movement. To Arnold its sectarian tendencies were paramount. In this respect Arnold thought that the Oxford Movement was little different from the Dissenters, who carved for themselves a religious preserve within the life of the nation and let most of the wider issues go to the devil or anyonc clsc who would take them. Sectarians were enemies of the Church in the wide, national sense in which Arnold understood the Church.

The Church of England to-day still stands under Arnold's criticism. Its declining position in the nation shown in its membership statistics, its shortage of clergy with recruitment behind losses, and increasingly alien culture in the nation as a whole, although it retains much of its Christian heritage, all press the Church into withdrawal and retrenchment. Much of the best thought in the Church to-day goes into promoting such withdrawal and retrenchment, but if it is done for its own sake and not to strengthen the Church for its task of Christianizing the nation, it comes under Arnold's fire.

Arnold will have nothing of the Church for its own sake. He is against any religious life apart from the world. The Church is an instrument to promote certain ends in the world, to Christianize the nation, inform the institutions of society with Christian principles and conscience and to bring approximations of the Kingdom of God. Arnold would agree with some recent words of Dr Kraemer: "The Church is provisional, not definitive. Consequently, the Church does not primarily exist on behalf of itself, but on behalf of the world."[6]

The Church is a missionary instrument. From this springs Arnold's passionate concern for unity. To-day the close relationship of mission and unity is a truism in most Churches; on a world level the integration of the International Missionary Council and the World Council of Churches is its symbol. This "rapprochement" is in the spiritual descent of Arnold, who put searching questions to the Churches of his day about their obligations to mission and unity. Then the questions were evaded; to-day they have not all been answered.

To-day unity and co-operation between the Churches

[6] H. Kraemer, *A Theology of the Laity,* Lutterworth Press, 1958, p. 127.

receive more attention than in Arnold's day, but it is doubtful whether mission, for all the talk about it, is implemented in the effective way in which Arnold desired. To Christianize the nation, when it is a complex industrial society, requires great flexibility of structure, new and changing structures for new and changing situations. It requires carefully planned deployment of men and resources into these new structures of mission. In a complex society the points of mission lie outside the grasp of the traditional parochial structure of the Church, adequate in a primitive agricultural society to embrace almost all aspects of life and now adequate only to embrace the home and family. To implement mission in Arnold's sense means to evolve structures of the Church which touch the functional aspects of life, government, work, industry with its many associated bodies, political parties, and the many other organizations and institutions necessary for the good health of an industrial society. Missionary thinking and action on this level of function are not yet abundant nor notable, with some exceptions, for good quality, at a time when good quality of thinking and action is vital. The insights of Arnold into the missionary situation of the newly emerged industrial society of the nineteenth century would point the missionary thinking and action of to-day in the right direction.

In conclusion, before liberating the reader for Arnold's own *Principles of Church Reform* we may quote a recent judgement: "Historians of the Oxford Movement in the Church of England are fond of quoting Dr Arnold's dictum, 'The Church, as it now stands, no human power can save', as though subsequent history had refuted it. But the saying was true then and it is true now."[7] We do well to heed Arnold's insistence on the Church's own self-criticism, its self-reforming, flexible, and instrumental nature in the interests of its mission to society in all its aspects, and to

[7] A. R. Vidler, *Essays in Liberality,* S.C.M., 1957, p. 19.

reinterpret that insistence for our own time. As a missionary theologian with sociological insights, Arnold can well be a guide to the Church of the mid twentieth century. We may conclude with a final quotation: "Thomas Arnold out-thought the Church of his day by generations, and not yet have we matched his teaching."[8]

[8] E. R. Wickham, *Church and People in an Industrial City,* p. 86.

Principles of Church Reform

CONTENTS

NOTE

The chapters, the subheadings, and the notes on pp. 170-1, referred to by number in the text, are added by the editors. The footnotes are Arnold's.

PREFACE

I HAVE called the following pamphlet, "Principles of Church Reform," because I thought it better to try to establish these, than to lose myself and my readers in a mass of minute details. For if the principles be true, there are persons of much greater experience and knowledge than myself to contrive the best way of carrying them into effect; while, had I proposed any particular arrangements which might have been ill-judged or impracticable, this error in the details might have been transferred by unfairness or ignorance to the main principles of the argument, and they would have been called impracticable also. These principles I believe to be irrefragable; that a Church Establishment is essential to the well-being of the nation; that the existence of Dissent impairs the usefulness of an Establishment always, and now, from peculiar circumstances, threatens its destruction; and that to extinguish Dissent by persecution being both wicked and impossible, there remains the true, but hitherto untried way, to extinguish it by comprehension; that different tribes should act together as it were in one army, and under one command, yet should each retain the arms and manner of fighting with which habit has made them most familiar.

But as to the manner of carrying these principles into effect, I am far from proposing any thing with equal confidence. Nor am I anxious about any particular measure, which I may have ventured to recommend, if any thing can be suggested by others, which may effect the same great object more completely. But practical ability, of which we have no lack in the country, must labour not merely for no good, but for absolute mischief, unless it clearly understands the principles of the question. And the numerous plans of Church Reform already before the public, have also the same bad effect, that they lead their readers off on a false scent, and make them fancy, that by their adoption the Church would be reformed and secured, when its great defects and dangers would remain in fact untouched. But the natural tendency of mankind to reform by patching rather than effectually, gives great reason to fear that some one or other of these plans will be adopted; and that the matter will then be considered by the Government to be set at rest. Whereas, in fact, it will not be at rest; but will be agitated with more violence than ever, and with less hope of a favourable settlement;—because one party will be exasperated at what they will call a mere mockery of Reform, and the other will complain that their concessions have given no satisfaction, and will therefore be disposed, for the time to come, to fight out the battle to the last.

RYDAL,
January 9th, 1833.

I

THE SITUATION

TRUE AND FALSE REFORM OF THE CHURCH

EVERY man who talks, writes, or votes in favour of Church Reform, would do well to ask himself, why he wishes for it. And in like manner the Government, when legislating to satisfy the general call for Church Reform, would do well to consider with what motives it is called for; to see, first, whether they who call the loudest are persons who ought to be satisfied; and, secondly, what it is that truth and wisdom demand; for their call ought certainly to be listened to, though it is generally preferred in a voice so gentle, that they who care not for it may easily avoid hearing it at all.

Now Church Reform being a very vague term, it is of great consequence to know what they, who use it, mean by it. It is impossible that a man can care, properly speaking, about the reform of any institution, if the objects of the institution are of no interest to him. If then a man, without being a Dissenter, is one who seldom or never goes to Church, and appears to have very little value for Christianity personally; the main object of the institution of the Church is clearly of no interest to him; and his anxiety for its reform can only be for the sake of certain subordinate objects which he may suppose to be promoted by it. Still if he be a man of enlarged and liberal views, and capable of desiring the intellectual welfare of his countrymen, and their moral improvement also so far as it affects society, he may sincerely wish to see the Church reformed in the proper sense of the term, although he may not be a religious man; because the social improvement of man is one of the direct objects of a Church establishment, although not its highest object; and it is properly to wish an institution reformed, if we wish it rendered more capable of effecting any of its proper objects. But men of another stamp, who neither value the social nor the religious benefits conferred by an establishment, cannot rightly be said to desire its reform; they merely wish to see it destroyed; and destruction is so very different from reform, that it is a gross fraud to call ourselves friends of the one, when what we really desire is the other.

Here then is one class of Church Reformers, and another class who call themselves by the same name, but whose proper title is Church Destroyers. A third, and a very numerous class, must however be added; men who have no value for the objects of the Church, nor yet any antipathy to it; who in point of fact neither wish for its reform nor for its destruction. They merely look upon its revenues as affording the means of lessening their outgoings in money, by being made in part available to public purposes. These men are in truth Church destroyers, only they are restrained by temper or by some scruple of conscience from going the full length of their own principles. Their object in short is wholly and entirely selfish, and if we might borrow the language of the seventeenth century, we might fitly distinguish them by the name of the "Self-seekers".

The avowed Dissenters join also in the call for Church Reform; and they again use the term with singular impropriety. They can hardly care about the reform of an institution from which they have altogether separated themselves. They belong, in fact, either to the class of Church Destroyers, or of Self-seekers: to the former, if being convinced that an establishment is an evil, they wish to see it altogether put down: to the latter, if their object be simply to be relieved from Church rates, Easter dues, and tithes, because they support a ministry of their own. But I have heard as yet no language from the Dissenters which could entitle them justly to the name of Church Reformers. That they may, and ought to become so, I shall endeavour to show hereafter.

Now it is manifest, that if we take all these classes of persons to the letter of their present,—perhaps I ought to say, their yesterday's language,—if we do reform the Church, by ridding it of the evils most loudly clamoured against, three out of four of them will still be unsatisfied. It is quite idle to think that the Destroyers, or the Self-seekers, really care about pluralities and non-residence, and the inequality of Church benefices: still less are they concerned about alterations in the Liturgy, or the introduction of a more effective clerical discipline. The real question with them is one of money,—they want a cheap religion,—and they lay the more stress upon the epithet, in proportion to their ignorance of the value of the article for which they are bargaining; about religion they know and care little,—about money they know and care much.

We are told that there is now an universal wish for Church Reform. This, as I have shown, is not true; on the contrary, I doubt exceedingly, whether the friends of Reform are powerful enough to get their object effected. There is on one side a great wish for Church destruction and Church robbery; and on the other side a great unwillingness to correct Church abuses: but the generality of the wish for Church Reform is a fact which I should exceedingly rejoice to see established.

It is not enough, in times like these, to stand battling about a few points of detail. We must take up the whole question from the beginning, that we may know on what grounds we are going to legislate. Before I discuss any scheme of Church Reform, I must state why I am utterly opposed to all schemes of Church destruction.

I will not insult even the most violent Church destroyer,

so far as to suppose him to contemplate the ejectment of the present holders of benefices. As the law declares that a man's benefice is his freehold, it is precisely the same thing to deprive an incumbent of the income arising from his church preferment, as to deprive any other individual of the rents of his land, or of the profits of his trade. If, therefore, such an act could be committed, it would be neither more nor less than literal robbery; and we should be far advanced on our way towards that happy consummation, when every man will keep what he can, and take what he can.

The Case for a Church Establishment

But, saving all existing interests, why should not the Establishment expire with the present generation? Why should not the tithes, in every parish, revert, on the next vacancy, to the several owners of the soil; and all Church lands be sold for the payment of the national debt; leaving the next generation of ministers, if there be any, to be maintained by the voluntary contributions of their hearers?

I am so anxious to get to the very principles of the whole question, that I am contented to pass over all the particular and practical objections which might be made to such a scheme;—such as its invasion of the rights of the patrons of Church benefices; and the question how far episcopal or chapter lands, which certainly were never granted by the state, could justly be taken by the state for its own purposes. These are all very substantial objections, and would, I hope, be fully insisted upon by all friends to law and right, if ever the proposal of Church destruction should come before the legislature in its plain form: but I hold it much more satisfactory, to rest the case simply on general principles; and to show that if the Establishment could be subverted, without the least individual injustice or illegality, still it would be the greatest possible folly in the nation to subvert it.

It is quite manifest, that the whole amount of Church property in England, including under that name, both tithes, so far as they are in clerical hands, and Church lands of every description, is so much saved out of the scramble of individual selfishness, and set apart for ever for public purpose.(1) Now there are few things from which society in England has suffered greater evil, than from the want of property so reserved: it is apparent in every town, and in every village, in the absence of public walks, public gardens, public exercise grounds, public museums, &c., in the former; and in most instances, of even so much as a common green, in the latter: let a man go where he will, he is beset on every side by the exclusiveness of private property; the public has kept nothing. This has arisen very much out of the false and degrading notions of civil society which have prevailed within the last century. Society has been regarded as a mere collection of individuals, looking each after his own interest; and the business of government has been limited to that of a mere police, whose sole use is to hinder these individuals from robbing or knocking each other down. This view of society, alike unphilosophical and unchristian, has largely counteracted the good which the world in this advanced stage of its existence, has derived from its increased experience; and its pernicious effects have been abundantly shown in the actual state of the poor throughout England. For their physical distresses, their ignorance, and their vices, are the true fruits of the system of "letting alone"; in other words, of leaving men to practise for their own advancement, all arts, save actual violence; of allowing every natural, and every artificial superiority, to enjoy and push its advantages to the utmost, and of suffering the weaker to pay the full penalty of their inferiority.

Thus, even before I consider the particular application of Church property, I hold it to be an enormous benefit that it is so much secured for ever to public uses;—a something saved out of the scramble, which no covetousness can appropriate, and no folly waste. Again, it is not only a considerable mass so saved;—but it is so happily divided, that every portion of the kingdom, with certain wretched exceptions, shares in the benefit. The sight of a church tower, wherever it is met with, is an assurance that every thing has not been bought up for private convenience or enjoyment;—that there is some provision made for public purposes, and for the welfare of the poorest and most destitute human being who lives within the hearing of its bells. In the most unattractive districts of the country, no less than in the most inviting, this same beneficent provision extends itself:—or if it does not, it is owing wholly to the neglect of these later times, when all things have been left to find their own level; and the result has been, as might well have been expected from the inequalities of the bottom, an alternation of some deep pools here and there with huge wastes of unmoistened sand and gravel.

But what are the particular public purposes for which this property is set apart? Alms-houses are an admirable provision for the poor and aged;—hospitals for the sick;—schools for the young;—a public garden furnishes amusement to all;—a public library gives instruction to all. But this property is designed to provide a benefit higher and more universal than any of these,—to secure for every parish the greatest blessing of human society, that is, the constant residence of one individual, who has no other business than to do good of every kind to every person. Men in general have their own profession or trade to follow; and although they are useful to society, yet it is but an indirect benefit—not intended for society in the first place, but for themselves; so that no one feels obliged to them for their services, because there is nothing in them which partakes of the nature of a kindness. Those again who possess an independent fortune, are not only raised too high to be in perfect sympathy with the majority of their neighbours, but are exposed to moral temptations of a peculiar kind, which often render them an inadequate example to others. Whereas, it is impossible to conceive a man placed so favourably for attaining to the highest perfection of our nature, as a parochial minister. Apart from all personal and particular interests; accustomed by his education and habits to take the purest and highest views of human life, and bound by his daily business to cherish and sweeten these by the charities of the kindest social intercourse: in delicacy and liberality of feeling on a level with the highest; but in rank and fortune standing in a position high enough to insure respect, yet not so high as to forbid sympathy:—with none of the harshness of legal authority, yet with a moral influence such as no legal authority could give:—ready to advise, when advice is called for, but yet more useful by the indirect counsel continually afforded by his conduct, his knowledge, his temper, and his manners;—he stands amidst the fever and selfishness of the world, as one whom the tainted atmosphere cannot harm, although he is for ever walking about in it, to abate its malignant power over its victims.

Now I wish it to be observed, that all this good results simply from the circumstance, that here is a man of education, relieved from the necessity of following any trade or ordinary profession in order to maintain himself, and placed in the most improving of all situations,—a life of constant intercourse with men, of which the direct and acknowledged business is to do them good physically and morally. Thus much is independent of religion:—and had there been a resident sophist stationed in every village of the Roman empire, with such a general commission to improve in every way the condition of the people, the amount of crime and misery would have been enormously lessened. But to all this, how much is superadded in the Christian ministry! How great is the difference of the notions conveyed by the terms "lecturer" and "preacher"; by the names of "sophist" and "pastor"! The truth is, that men bear impatiently the teaching of men, unless it comes with more than man's authority: the beneficent relations in which a minister stands towards his people, derive much of their power from this very circumstance, that he is a minister of *religion*. And Christianity, whilst it fully invests him with this character, yet has provided in the strongest manner against superstition and priestcraft; for a minister can speak with no authority beyond his commission, and this commission lies open for all men, to judge whether he adheres to it or no. It gives him power unspeakable, so long as he faithfully discharges it: but deserts and condemns him the very moment that he would pervert it to selfish purposes, to make his own word a law, and himself an idol. But in this commission there is contained indeed the very food, and more than the food of man's life: the remedy for all troubles and sorrows, from the simplest physical suffering of the rudest nature, up to the mental conflicts which are the inevitable portion of the loftiest and most sensitive: the medicine for all moral evil, from the mere bodily appetites of the most grossly ignorant, to the most delicate forms of pride or selfishness in minds of the highest intelligence: the light to clear up every perplexity of practice, strengthening the judgment through the purified affections: the most exalted hope inseparably united with the deepest humility; because we believe in Christ crucified—because we trust in Christ risen. I shall not be suspected of meaning this high character of the benefits of a national Christian ministry to apply in its full perfection to the actual state of the Church amongst us. The faults of human nature will always make the practice of an institution fall below its theory. But it is no less true that all the tendencies of the ministerial office, as such, are wholly beneficial; and if the actual good derived from it be not so great as it might be, this is owing to counteracting causes, some remediable—such, for instance, as faults produced by imperfect education and inefficient church discipline; others, arising out of the mere weakness of human nature, admitting only of palliation, not of complete removal.

Now an appropriation of a certain portion of property to secure for ever to a whole people so invaluable a blessing as a resident Christian ministry dispersed over every part of the country, will naturally be objected to by those who hate the very names of God and of goodness. And persons who arrive from mere brutishness at the same practical conclusion to which the godless party are led by deliberate wickedness,—men who can neither look before nor after, but limit their notions of political good to the mere physical welfare of their own generation, because they can understand nothing higher,—such persons may consistently think that hand work is more useful than head or heart work, and that no elements in society can be so well spared as piety, and charity, and moral wisdom. It is no wonder, then, but a just tribute to the excellence of the Christian ministry, that it should be hated by the sublimed and systematic wickedness of the godless party, and by the brute ignorance and coarseness of the dregs of the democracy. But that men who, though not religious, are yet admirers of much that is noble, and much that is excellent;—still more, that men who really fear God and love Christianity, should be found to doubt the wisdom of a national provision for the moral and intellectual improvement of the people, for giving them the knowledge of that truth which is life eternal,—this is on the face of it a phenomenon so strange, nay, so monstrous, that we cannot but eagerly desire, for the honour of human nature, to explain the causes of it.

Unity and Sectarianism

It has arisen from that worst reproach of the Christian name,—the spirit of sectarianism. For Christians having become divided into a thousand sects, and refusing to join in each other's worship, a national establishment is regarded as an unjust preference of one sect over another;—and, as it is considered impossible to establish all, and unfair to establish any other rather than another, there remains no alternative but to establish none; and, to use a phrase much in fashion, to look upon every man's religion as an affair between God and his own conscience only.

That the objection to a national provision for the ministers of religion arises, amongst thinking men, solely out of the difficulties created by sectarianism, is manifest from this;—that where sectarianism has not existed, or only in an insignificant degree, the wisdom of such a provision has been allowed with remarkable unanimity. For, not to speak of the ancient world, where it was a thing unheard of for a state to be without its national worship, its temples, its festivals, and its priests; the whole Christian world, from the time that governments have become Christian, has acted uniformly on the same principle, with the single exception of the United States of America, where the evil spirit of sectarianism has wrought his perfect work. And what is still more to our purpose, the French people, even while declaring that they will have no established religion, have yet retained the great benefit of an establishment, namely, a national provision for the religious instruction of the people, inasmuch as they keep up the churches, and pay the ministers who officiate in them.(2) This they do, because the clear wisdom of the principle is not obscured to their minds by the perplexities which rise out of religious dissent;—the Catholics are so great a majority, and in most parts of France so nearly the whole of the population, that Catholic and Christian are convertible terms, and the state's wish to instruct its people is not frustrated by the endless discussions of contending sects, each objecting to all forms of instruction but its own.

This evil of religious dissent is so enormous,—is so fraught with danger at this moment to our highest interests, national and spiritual,—and has been to my mind so unfairly and unsatisfactorily treated by men of all parties, that I shall make no apology for entering fully upon the consideration of it. Unless it be duly appreciated, and in some measure remedied, it is perfectly needless to talk of Church Reform.

Whoever is acquainted with Christianity, must see that differences of opinion amongst Christians are absolutely unavoidable. First, because our religion being a thing of the deepest personal interest, we are keenly alive to all the great questions connected with it, which was not the case with heathenism. Secondly, these questions are exceedingly numerous, inasmuch as our religion affects our whole moral being, and must involve, therefore, a great variety of metaphysical, moral, and political points;—that is to say, those very points which, lying out of the reach of demonstrative science, are, through the constitution of man's nature, peculiarly apt to be regarded by different minds differently. And thirdly, although all Christians allow the Scriptures to be of decisive authority, whenever their judgment is pronounced on any given case, yet the peculiar form of these Scriptures, which in the New Testament is rather that of a commentary than of a text; the critical difficulties attending their interpretation, and the still greater difficulty as to their application:—it being a constant question whether such and such rules, and still more whether such and such recorded facts or practices, were meant to be universally binding;—and it being a farther question, amidst the infinite variety of human affairs, whether any case, differing more or less in its circumstances, properly comes under the scope of any given Scripture rule;—all these things prevent the Scriptures from being in practice decisive on controverted points, because the contending parties, while alike acknowledging the judge's authority, persist in putting a different construction upon the words of his sentence.

Aware of this state of things, and aware also with characteristic wisdom, of the deadly evil of religious divisions, the

Roman Catholic Church ascribed to the sovereign power in the Christian society, in every successive age, an infallible spirit of truth, whereby the real meaning of any disputed passage of Scripture might be certainly and authoritatively declared; and if the Scripture were silent, then the living voice of the Church might supply its place,—and being guided by that same spirit which had inspired the written word, might pronounce upon any new point of controversy with a decision of no less authority.

With the same view of preventing divisions, the unity of the Church was maintained, in a sense perfectly intelligible and consistent. Christians, wherever they lived, belonged literally to one and the same society,—they were subject to the same laws and to the same government. National and political distinctions were wholly lost sight of; the vicar of Christ and his general council knew nothing of England or of France, of Germany or of Spain; they made laws for *Christendom*—a magnificent word, and well expressing those high and consistent notions of unity, on which the Church of Rome based its system. One government, one law, one faith, kept free from doubt and error by the support of an infallible authority—the theory was in perfect harmony with itself, and most imposing from its beauty and apparent usefulness; but it began with assuming a falsehood, and its intended conclusion was an impossibility.

It is false that there exists in the Church any power or office endowed with the gift of infallible wisdom; and therefore it is impossible to prevent differences of opinion. But the claim to infallibility was not only false, but mischievous; because it encouraged the notion that these differences were to be condemned and prevented, and thus hindered men from learning the truer and better lesson, how to make them perfectly compatible with Christian union. Doubtless it were a far happier state of things if men did not differ from each other at all;—but this may be wished for only; it is a serious folly to expect it. For so, while grieving over an inevitable evil, we heap on it aggravations of our own making, which are far worse than the original mischief. Differences of opinion will exist, but it is our fault that they should have been considered equivalent to differences of principle, and made a reason for separation and hostility.

Our fathers rightly appreciated the value of church unity; but they strangely mistook the means of preserving it. Their system consisted in drawing up a statement of what they deemed important truths, and in appointing a form of worship and a ceremonial which they believed to be at once dignified and edifying; and then they proposed to oblige every man, by the dread of legal penalties or disqualifications, to subscribe to their opinions, and to conform to their rites and practices. But they forgot that while requiring this agreement, they had themselves disclaimed, what alone could justify them in enforcing it—the possession of infallibility. They had parted with the weapon which would have served them most effectually, and strange were the expedients resorted to for supplying its place. At one time it was the Apostles' Creed; at another, the decrees of the four first general councils; or, at another, the general consent of the primitive Church, which formed an authoritative standard of such truths as might not be questioned without heresy. But though the elephant might still rest upon the tortoise, and the tortoise on the stone, yet since the claim to infallibility was once abandoned, the stone itself rested on nothing. The four first councils were appealed to as sanctioning their interpretation of Scripture by men who yet confessed that the decisions of these councils were only of force, because they were agreeable to the Scripture. Turn which ever way they would, they sought in vain for an *authority* in religious controversies; infallibility being nowhere to be found, it was merely opinion against opinion; and however convinced either party might be of the truth of its own views, they had no right to judge their opponents.

With regard to the ceremonies and practices of the Church, a different ground was taken. It is curious to observe the contradictory positions in which the two parties were placed:—the Church of England enforcing a tyranny upon principles in themselves most liberal and most true; —the Dissenters accidentally advocating the cause of liberty, while their principles were those of the most narrow-minded fanaticism. One feels ashamed to think that the great truths so clearly and so eloquently established by Hooker, in the earlier books of his ecclesiastical polity, should have served in practice the petty tyranny of Laud and Whitgift, or the utterly selfish and worldly policy of Elizabeth. The Church of England maintained most truly, that rites and ceremonies, being things indifferent in themselves, might be altered according to the difference of times and countries, and that the regulation of such matters was left wholly to the national Church. But inasmuch as the government of the national Church was a mere despotism—the crown having virtually transferred to itself the authority formerly exercised by the popes—its appointments were made with an imperious stiffness, which was the more offensive from the confessed indifferent nature of the matters in question; and while one ritual was inflexibly imposed upon the whole community, in direct opposition to the feelings of many of its members, and too simple and unattractive to engage the sympathies of the multitude, this fond attempt to arrive at uniformity, inflicted a deadly blow, according to Lord Falkland's (3) most true observation on the real blessing of Christian union.

I am well aware that if it be a mere question of comparative faultiness, the opponents of the Established Church in the sixteenth and seventeenth centuries are at least as much to be condemned as its rulers. That coarse-minded ignorance, which delighted to isolate itself from all the noble recollections of past times, and confounded all the institutions and practices of the Christian Church during several centuries, under the opprobrious names of superstition and idolatry; that captious superstition which quarrelled with the form of a minister's cap, or the colour of his dress, deserved indeed little consideration, if the principles of government are to be made dependent on the merits of particular parties or individuals. But the cause of truth, and the welfare of mankind, have been for ever sacrificed to the paltry triumphs of personal argument:—if a party can show that its opponents have been more blameable than itself, it looks upon itself as standing clear in the judgment of posterity and of God. The provocation given may indeed lessen our estimate of the guilt of individuals; but it ought not to affect our sentiments of the wisdom or evil tendency of their conduct; and though the virulence and ignorance of the puritans may dispose us to excuse Whitgift and Laud, as individuals, yet their system is not the less to be condemned, as in itself arbitrary and schismatical, and tending to aggravate and perpetuate the evils which it professed to combat.

Thus within fifty years of the overthrow of the Roman Catholic religion in England, the spirit of Protestantism, followed up only in one half of its conclusions, had divided the nation into two hostile parties, each careless of union, and looking only to victory. The religious quarrel blending itself with the political struggle at which society in its progress had then arrived, became thus the more irreconcilable; each party boasted of its martyrs, and exulted in the judgments which had befallen its enemies; the royalist churchman consecrated the 29th of May as a day of national thanksgiving; the puritan, who had deemed popery and prelacy crushed for ever by the arms of God's saints, now bewailed the new St. Bartholomew of 1662, and the vindictive oppression of the Five Mile Act.

There succeeded an age of less zeal, but scarcely of more charity. Time had reconciled men to the monstrous sight of a large proportion of a Christian people living in a complete religious separation from their fellow-Christians; of a numerous portion of the children of the State, living as aliens from the national worship. And the means hitherto adopted for preventing such a division were so odious in themselves, and had so signally failed to effect their object, that none could wish them to be continued any longer. Hostilities were accordingly suspended, and the Toleration Act was passed;— a strange measure, by which the nation sanctioned the non-observance of its own institutions, and relaxed by one half the bond of national communion. Yet at the very same period an attempt to effect, not a peace, but an union with the Dissenters, totally failed: those true Christians who wished to make the national Church more comprehensive, were unable to carry their point: persecution first—toleration afterwards—any thing seemed preferable to Christian charity and Christian union.

Then followed one of those awful periods in the history of a nation, which may be emphatically called its times of trial. I mean those tranquil intervals between one great revolution and another, in which an opportunity is offered for profiting by the lessons of past experience, and to direct the course of the future for good. From our present dizzy state, it is startling to look back on the deep calm of the first seventy years of the eighteenth century. All the evils of society were yet manageable; while complete political freedom, and a vigorous state of mental activity, seemed to promise that the growth of good would more than keep pace with them, and that thus they might be kept down for ever. But tranquillity, as usual, bred carelessness; events were left to take their own way uncontrolled; the weeds grew fast, while none thought of sowing the good seed. The Church and the Dissenters lived in peace; but their separation became daily more confirmed. Meanwhile the uniformity, and the strict formality, which the Church had fondly adopted in order to extinguish Dissent, now manifestly encouraged it. As the population increased, and began to congregate into large masses in those parts of the country which before had been thinly inhabited, the Church required an enlarged machinery, at once flexible, and powerful. What she had was both stiff and feeble; her ministers could only officiate in a church, and were compelled to confine themselves to the prescribed forms of the liturgy; while the Dissenters, free and unrestricted, could exercise their ministry as circumstances required it, whether in a mine, by a canal side, or at the doors of a manufactory; they could join in hymns with their congregations, could pray, expound the Scriptures, exhort, awaken, or persuade, in such variety and in such proportions as the time, the place, the mood of their hearers, or their own, might suggest or call for.

Thus, by the very nature of the case, the influence of the Dissenters spread amongst the poorer classes. It was a great good, that the poor and ignorant should receive any knowledge of Christianity;—but it was a mixed good, because the evil of sectarianism was at hand to taint it. The minister at the meeting-house rejoiced to thin the church; —the minister of the church rejoiced in his turn, if he could win back hearers from the meeting. As if their great common cause had not required all their efforts, much of their zeal was directed against each other; and if there was not hostility, there was an increase of rivalry and of jealousy. It might have been thought that the many good and active men who were now daily rising up amongst the ministers of the Establishment, would have been struck by the evils of their position, and have laboured to remove them. But some had been so used to the existence of Dissent, that they were insensible to the magnitude of its evils; —others, with the old party spirit of the High Churchmen, imagined that all the blame of the separation rested with the Dissenters; they talked of the sin of schism, as if they were not equally guilty of it; they would have rejoiced in the conformity of the opposite party, that is to say, in their own victory; but they had no notion of any thing like a fair union. Others, again, fully occupied with their own individual duties, and feeling that they themselves were usefully employed, never directed their attention to the inadequacy of the system to which they belonged, considered as a whole; while a fourth set argued against reforming the Church now, from the fact of its having gone unreformed so long; and because the crisis was not yet arrived, they were blind to the sure symptoms of its progress, and believed that it would only be brought on by the means used to avert it.

But the population outgrew the efforts both of the Church and of the Dissenters; and multitudes of persons existed in the country who could not properly be said to belong to either. These were, of course, the most ignorant and degraded portion of the whole community,—a body whose influence is always for evil of some sort, but not always for evil of the same sort,—which is first the brute abettor and encourager of abuses, and afterwards their equally brute destroyer. For many years the populace hated the Dissenters for the strictness of their lives, and because they had departed from the institutions of their country; for ignorance, before it is irritated by physical distress, and thoroughly imbued with the excitement of political agitation, is blindly averse to all change, and looks upon reform as a trouble and a disturbance. Thus the populace in Spain and in Naples have shown themselves decided enemies to the constitutional party; and thus the mob at Birmingham, so late as the year 1791, plundered and burnt houses to the cry of "Church and King", and threatened to roast Dr. Priestley (4) alive, as a heretic. But there is a time, and it is one fraught with revolutions, when this tide of ignorance suddenly turns and runs in the opposite direction with equal violence. Distress and continued agitation produce this change; but its peculiar danger arises from this, that its causes operate for a long time without any apparent effect, and we observe their seeming inefficiency till we think that there is nothing to fear from them; when suddenly the ground falls in under our feet, and we find that their work, though slow, had been done but too surely. And this is now the case with the populace of England. From cheering for Church and King, they are now come to cry for no bishops, no tithes, and no rates: from persecuting the Dissenters, because they had separated from the Church, they are now eagerly joining with them for that very same reason; while the Dissenters, on their part, readily welcome these new auxiliaries, and reckon on their aid for effecting the complete destruction of their old enemy.

This being the state of things, it is evident, that the existence of Dissent has divided the efforts of Christians, so as to make them more adverse to each other than to the cause of ungodliness and wickedness; it has prevented the nation from feeling the full benefits of its national Establishment, and now bids fair to deprive us of them altogether. Dissent, indeed, when it becomes general, makes the Establishment cease to be national; there being so large a portion of the nation whose religious wants it does not satisfy. Yet we have seen, on the other hand, that differences of religious opinion, and of religious rites and ceremonies, are absolutely unavoidable; and that since there exists on earth no infallible authority to decide controversies between Christians, it is vain for any one sect to condemn another, or in its dealings with others to assume that itself is certainly right, and its opponents as certainly in error.

Is it not, then, worth while to try a different system? And since disunion is something so contrary to the spirit of Christianity, and difference of opinion a thing so inevitable to human nature, might it not be possible to escape the former without the folly of attempting to get rid of the latter; to constitute a Church thoroughly national, thoroughly united, thoroughly Christian, which should allow great varieties of opinion, and of ceremonies, and forms of worship, according to the various knowledge, and habits, and tempers of its members, while it truly held one common faith, and trusted in one common Saviour and worshipped one common God?

2

A UNITED, COMPREHENSIVE CHURCH

Unity of Belief

The problem then is, to unite in one Church different opinions and different rites and ceremonies; and first, let us consider the case of a difference of religious opinions.

Before such an union is considered impracticable, or injurious to the cause of Christianity, might we not remember what, and how many, those points are, on which all Christians are agreed?

We all believe in one God, a spiritual and all-perfect Being, who made us, and all things; who governs all things by His Providence; who loves goodness, and abhors wickedness.

We all believe that Jesus Christ, His Son, came into the world for our salvation; that He died, and rose again from the dead, to prove that His true servants shall not die eternally, but shall rise as He is risen, and enjoy an eternal life with Him and with His Father.

We all believe that the volume of the Old and New Testaments contains the revelation of God's will to man; that no other revelation than what is there recorded has been ever given to mankind before or since; that it is a standard of faith and a rule of practice; so that we all acknowledge its authority, although we may often understand its meaning differently.

We all have, with very few exceptions, the same notions of right and wrong; or, at any rate, the differences on these points do not exist between Christians of different sects, but between sincere Christians of all sects, and those who are little better than mere Christians in name. We all hold that natural faults are not therefore excusable, but are earnestly to be struggled against; that pride and sensuality are amongst the worst sins; that self-denial, humility, devotion, and charity, are amongst the highest virtues. We all believe that our first great duty is to love God; our second, to love our neighbour.

Now, considering that on these great points all Christians are agreed, while they differ on most of them from all who are not Christians, does it seem unreasonable that persons so united in the main principles of man's life, in the objects of their religious affections, and of their hopes for eternity, should be contented to live with one another as members of the same religious society?

But they differ also in many important points, and cannot therefore form one church without seeming to sanction what they respectively believe to be error. Now, setting aside the different opinions on church government, which I shall notice presently, is it true that there are many important points of pure doctrine on which the great majority of Christians in England at this moment are not agreed? The Presbyterians, the Methodists of all denominations, the Independents, the Baptists, the Moravians, can hardly be said to differ on any important point, except as connected with church government, either from one another or from the Establishment. The difference with the Baptists as to the lawfulness of Infant Baptism, may perhaps be thought an exception; but, if I mistake not, one of the highest authorities among the Baptists has expressly maintained the lawfulness of communion with Pædobaptists; and the question is not which practice is the more expedient, but whether Infant Baptism on the one hand, or the refusing it to all who cannot understand its meaning on the other, be either of them errors so fatal as to make it impossible to hold religious communion with those who maintain them.

There remain the Quakers, the Roman Catholics, and the Unitarians, whose differences appear to offer greater difficulty. And undoubtedly, so long as these sects preserve exactly their present character, it would seem impracticable to comprehend them in any national Christian church; the epithet "national" excluding the two former, and the epithet "Christian," rendering alike impossible the admission of the latter. But the harshest and most offensive part of the peculiarities of every sect has always arisen from the opposition of antagonists. Extravagance in one extreme provokes equal extravagance in the other. If, then, instead of devising forms so positive and controversial, as to excite mistrust of their accuracy in the most impartial minds, and vehement opposition from those whose opinions lean to a different side, we were to make our language general and comprehensive, and content ourselves with protesting against the abuses which may follow from an exclusive view of the question, even when it is in itself substantially true, it is probable that those who differ from us would soon begin to consider the subject in a different temper; and that if truth were the object of both parties, and not victory, truth would in fact be more nearly attained by both. In this respect, the spirit of the Seventeenth Article of the Church of England affords an excellent model, inasmuch as it is intended to be comprehensive and conciliatory, rather than controversial. And the effect to be hoped for from assuming such a tone, would be the bringing reasonable and moderate men to meet us, and to unite with us; there would of course be always some violent spirits, who would maintain their peculiar tenets without modification; but the end of all wise government, whether in temporal matters or in spiritual, is not to satisfy every body, which is impossible, but to make the dissatisfied a powerless minority, by drawing away from them that mass of curable discontent whose support can alone make them dangerous.

That there is this tractable disposition in the majority of mankind, experience sufficiently proves. And we should remember that at present the spirit of sectarianism binds many men even to the extravagancies of their own party, because they think it a point of honour not to be suspected of lukewarmness. But even as things are, we know that many Quakers conform, in their dress and language, much more nearly to the rest of the world, than the stricter members of their sect approve of. Would not this temper be carried still further if those needless assertions of the lawfulness of war and of oaths were expunged from our Articles, and if we showed ourselves more sensible to that high conception of Christian perfection, which breathes through their whole system, and which, even when perverted into extravagance, ought not to be spoken of without respect?

Again, with the Roman Catholics;—as long as we indulge in that scurrilous language respecting them, which is almost habitual to one party amongst us, we shall assuredly do nothing but confirm them in all their errors, and increase their abhorrence of Protestantism. It is perfectly idle to attack their particular tenets and practices, till we can persuade them, that they may lawfully judge for themselves. Nor shall we effect this by calling the Pope antichrist;—and his claim to infallibility the blasphemous fruit of ambition and avarice. We dare not analyse too closely the motives of our best actions;—but if ever grand conceptions of establishing the dominion of good over evil may be allowed to have concealed from the heart the ignobler feelings which may have been mixed with them, this excuse may justly be pleaded for Gregory VII and Innocent III. The infallibility of the Church was the fond effort of the human mind to believe in the reality of the support which its weakness so needed;—its unity was a splendid dream, beautiful but impracticable. We might sympathize with the Roman Catholics in the wish that we could find any infallible guide—that there existed on earth the wisdom and the goodness capable of exercising an universal dominion;—and then we might urge them to consider whether indeed our wishes are enough to warrant our belief—whether experience does not forbid the fulfilment of our hopes;—and whether the lesser, but certain good, be not a surer stay to our infirmities, than an image of perfection which we cannot realize.

If ever the Roman Catholics could be convinced that universal empire is equally impracticable in religious matters as in temporal; and that no bond of society, using the term in the strict sense of a body of men living under the same government, and bound by the same laws, can be more extensive than that of the political society or nation to which every man belongs by birth, they would then feel that they were members naturally of the Church of England, and not of the Church of central Italy. And then they would acknowledge further, that as the Parliaments of our ancestors could not preclude their posterity from making such alterations as the altered circumstances of a future generation might demand; so neither could the councils of our ancestors debar their successors from a similar right; that the national Church in every generation is equally invested with sovereign power to order such rites and forms of worship as it may deem expedient; and that though necessarily unable to command conviction in matters of opinion, it may yet lawfully regulate matters of practice. And if our Church were made truly national in point of government, if the king's supremacy were made what it was intended to be in principle, the substitution of a domestic government instead of a foreign one, and if our ecclesiastical constitution were rendered definite and intelligible, is it beyond hope, that many who are now Roman Catholics, would ere long unite themselves religiously as well as politically with the rest of their countrymen?

Lastly, with regard to the Unitarians, it seems to me that in their case an alteration of our present terms of communion would be especially useful. The Unitarian body in England consists of elements the most dissimilar; including many who merely call themselves Unitarians, because the name of unbeliever is not yet thought creditable, and some also who are disgusted with their unchristian associates, but who cannot join a church which retains the Athanasian creed. Every means should be taken to separate these from their present unworthy society, that they who are really Christians might join their fellow-Christians, and they who are really unbelievers might be known by all the world to be so. I know that many good men draw a broad line of distinction between errors respecting the Trinity, and errors on any other point. They cannot unite, they say, with those who are not Trinitarians; and Lord Henley (5), while advocating an union with Dissenters in general, especially excepts those who, to use his own language, "deny the divinity of our Lord, or the mystery of the triune Jehovah". The last expression is worthy of notice, as affording a specimen of that irritating phraseology which has confirmed so many in error. Is it the way to reclaim any man from Unitarianism, to insist upon his believing in "the mystery of the triune Jehovah?" The real question is, not what theoretical articles a man will or will not subscribe to, but what essential parts of Christian worship he is unable to use. Now the addressing Christ in the language of prayer and praise, is an essential part of Christian worship. Every Christian would feel his devotions incomplete, if this formed no part of them. This, therefore, cannot be sacrificed; but we are by no means bound to inquire, whether all who pray to Christ entertain exactly the same ideas of his nature. I believe that Arianism involves in it some very erroneous notions as to the object of religious worship; but if an Arian will join in our worship of Christ, and will call him Lord and God, there is neither wisdom nor charity in insisting that he shall explain what he means by these terms; nor in questioning the strength and sincerity of his faith in his Saviour, because he makes too great a distinction between the divinity of the Father, and that which he allows to be the attribute of the Son.

It seems to have been the boast hitherto of the several sects of Christians, to invent formulæ both of worship and of creeds, which should serve as a test of any latent error; that is, in other words, which should force a man to differ from them, however gladly he would have remained in their communion. May God give us, for the time to come, a wiser and a better spirit; and may we think that the true problem to be solved in the composition of all articles and creeds and prayers for public use, is no other than this; how to frame them so as to provoke the least possible disagreement, without sacrificing, in our own practical worship, the expression of such feelings as are essential to our own edification.

If it be said that this is contrary to the uniform example of the Christian world, it is unhappily too true that it is so: and let history answer how the cause of Christianity has prospered under the system actually adopted. Or let those answer who, in attempting to acquaint themselves with ecclesiastical history, have groaned inwardly for very weariness at its dull and painful details. What ought to be more noble, or more beautiful, than the gradual progress of the Spirit of light and love, dispelling the darkness of folly, and subduing into one divine harmony all the jarring elements of evil, which divided amongst them the chaos of this world's empire? Such should have been the history of the Christian church; and what has it been actually? No steady and unwavering advance of heavenly spirits; but one continually interrupted, checked, diverted from its course, nay, driven backwards, as of men possessed by some bewildering spell—wasting their strength upon imaginary obstacles—fancying that their road lay to the right or left, when it led straight forward—hindering each other's progress and their own by stopping to analyse and dispute about the nature of the sun's light till all were blinded by it—instead of thankfully using its aid to show them the true path onward. In other words, men overrated the evil of difference of opinion, and underrated that of difference of practice; and their efforts were thus diverted from a cause in which all good men would have striven together, to one where goodness and wickedness were mere accidental adjuncts, equally found on one side as on the other. Or to take a much narrower view of the question, we should consider that the very notion of an extensive society implies a proportionate laxity in its points of union. There is a choice between entire agreement with a very few, or general agreement with many, or agreement in some particular points with all; but entire agreement with many, or general agreement with all, are things impossible. Two individuals might possibly agree in three hundred articles of religion; but as they add to their own numbers, they must diminish that of their articles, unless they can prevent their associates from exercising their own understandings. Nor is this only applicable to a national church; it holds good of the smallest districts, where there are assembled men of different habits, different abilities, different degrees of knowledge, different tempers, and it may be almost said different ages. If agreement of *opinion* on a number of points be required as the condition of communion, there must be many different churches in every town; and these will be continually multiplying, for exclusiveness grows by indulgence; and men will form select societies among the select, till the church of Christ will become almost infinitely divisible. Infallibility or brute ignorance can alone prevent differences of opinion. Men, at once fallible and inquiring, have their choice either of following these differences up into endless schisms, or of allowing them to exist together unheeded, under the true bond of agreement of principle.

I may be pardoned, perhaps, for some repetition in dwelling again on points already noticed; as this perversion of the term unity, from a practicable and useful sense to one at once impracticable and unimportant, has been the great mischief both of the Christian church in general, and of the Church of England in particular, and has brought about in the latter that monstrous state of things in which a total Reform can alone save it from total destruction.

Reforms in Church Government and Administration

We now proceed then to consider the practicability of uniting in one national church men attached to various forms of church government.

In proposing any alterations in this part of our system, we have at least this advantage;—that the present state of things is acceptable to no one. It is in fact a confessed anomaly, at once weak and unpopular; and it has come to such a point of actual dissolution, that it has been made a question what the government of the Church of England is. Yet there exist prejudices which would be more shocked, perhaps, by any change than they are by the present system; and these prejudices should be consulted as far as is possible, without interfering with the substantial ends of all government.

The Ministry

It is the fashion to complain of the great inequality which prevails in the Established Church; but it is not very difficult to prove that there is not inequality enough; —that the Church is like an army destitute of non-commissioned officers, and therefore incapable of acting with sufficient effect, through this defect in its organization. In other words, as all classes of society require the services of the ministers of religion, the ministry should contain persons taken from all; and in a national church, all the great divisions of the nation should have a share in the government. The Scotch Church fails in not reaching up to the level of the aristocracy;—the English Church, as Wesley saw, fails in not reaching down to the level of the poor;—the Roman Church, embracing in the wide range of its offices every rank of society, from the prince to the peasant, offers in this respect a perfect model. And if the scale of ascent be sufficiently gradual, the Christian ministry thus furnishes a beautiful chain to link the highest and the lowest together through the bond of their sacred office, without the absurdity of attempting to bring both to the same level.

But when we propose such a scale, we find that its highest and lowest points are vehemently objected to by opposite parties. On one side we have the old cry against prelacy, strengthened at this moment by a foolish political prejudice, and by the natural impatience of the lovers of evil at seeing Christianity advanced, as such, to situations of honour and influence. And on the other side, there is a dread of low-minded and uneducated teachers; combined, perhaps, with some Jewish and Pagan confusion of the Christian ministry with the caste and family priesthoods of antiquity. The cry against a wealthy and dignified episcopacy, is, where it is honest, the fruit of a whole series of mistakes and misconceptions. It is ridiculous to suppose, that the rulers of a society could ever have been, as a body, taken from the poorer members of it. The relation of the Apostles to the rest of the Church was wholly peculiar: men, so divinely gifted, had a claim to authority, which set aside all considerations of wealth or poverty; but the instant that these gifts ceased, wealth would be in itself a title to power; and where merit was equal, a rich man would have made a more efficient bishop than a poor one. St. Paul requires a bishop to be "given to hospitality"; he must therefore have wherewith to exercise it. There is a great deal said in the New Testament against covetousness and self-indulgence; but this is addressed to all Christians equally; and if a layman does not conceive himself to be violating these commands by possessing a considerable property, with what assurance can he press such an interpretation of them upon his neighbour, because he is a minister? Some who inveigh against the wealth of the Church, meaning by that term the clergy, and yet express great satisfaction in the wealth of the nation, which in this country is the Church, betray an ignorance and an inconsistency truly surprising: but an argument from misapplied texts of Scripture would be called superstition and folly, if it were urged in defence of tithes; and truly it is no less fanaticism and folly, or folly and something worse, when it is used against the riches of the clergy, than when it is used in support of them.

Equally unreasonable are the arguments against an order of ministers chosen from the poorer classes of society. That they must be generally less educated than the ministers of a richer class is clear; and so far they would be inferior to them: nor is it intended that an uneducated man should in any case be the principal minister in a parish, as that would undo one of the chief benefits, so far as moral and social improvement is concerned, of a national establishment. But there is an enormous advantage in giving all ranks of society their share in the administration of the Church: they would think that they had an interest in a system which provided a place for them as well as for the rich; but no man cares much about a system in which he is wholly passive; in which he never acts himself, but is always the object of the care and regulations of others. The difference of the gifts possessed by the first Christians, applies entirely, by analogy, to us now: "those members of the body, which seem to be more feeble, are necessary"; and more is gained by the variety of qualifications, than is lost by their inequality.

But it is said that uneducated ministers would spread the most mischievous fanaticism. I ask, what is the case as things are now? Have we no fanatical teaching at present? Now, if an uneducated man of serious impressions feels that he can be useful to persons of his own sort, by pressing on their minds the truths which have improved and comforted his own, he finds no place for himself in the Established Church. The clergyman of his parish would tell him to go to church and learn himself, instead of setting up to teach others. And no doubt he has enough to learn, but so have we all: and it does not follow that he should be unfit to teach some, because there are others who could teach him. But, meanwhile, the result is, that whether fit or not, he *does* teach: the Toleration Act has settled this point. He may teach where and what he chooses, so long as he does not belong to the Establishment. And of what use is it to say that the *Church* does not suffer from his ignorance, and is innocent of encouraging it? The *nation* suffers from it, so far as it is ignorance, and the National Church is therefore concerned in remedying it. At present it exists unchecked and undirected, because the Church abandons it to itself: but if it were incorporated into its system, it would become immediately subject to control, and whilst all, and more than all, of its present usefulness was derived from it, its mischiefs would in a great degree be obviated.

The Laity

But the most essential step towards effecting this and every other improvement in the Church, consists in giving to the laity a greater share in its ordinary government.

The Bishop stands alone in his diocese, the Minister in his parish; and so little are the laity associated with them officially in their operations, that the very word Church has lost its proper meaning, and is constantly used to express only the clerical members of it. The worst consequence of this, no doubt, is the unchristian distinction thus created between the clergy and the laity, to the equal injury of both; but one considerable evil resulting from it is the annihilation of Church discipline. As long as the clergy have the whole administration of the Church in their own hands, their power over other men must be neutralized, or else we incur all the dangers of a system of priestcraft; and for the same reason, if a Bishop be the sole ruler of his diocese, he must be so shackled to prevent him from becoming a tyrant, as to be actually divested of the powers essential to government. And so from a superstition about what men fancy to be the divine right of Episcopacy, the Church has practically all but gone to pieces, from the want of any government at all.

This want of government or of social organization in the Church, has been one main cause of the multiplication of Dissenters. Men's social wants have not been satisfied;—and a Christian Church which fails in this particular, neglects one of the most important ends of Christianity. Consider the case of one of the parishes in a large manufacturing town; there is a population of several thousand souls often comprised nominally within the same subdivision of the whole Christian society of the nation; but what is their organization and bond of union? Perhaps one parish church, utterly unable to contain a fourth part of their numbers;—and one minister, who must be physically incapable of becoming personally acquainted with even so much as a smaller proportion of them. The other officers of the parochial society are the parish clerk, the churchwardens, the overseers of the poor,—how little like the deacons of old,—the beadle, and the constable! What an organization for a religious society! And how natural was it that men should form distinct societies for themselves, when that to which they nominally belonged performed none of the functions of a society. And even in those cases where by the exertions of the incumbent in providing one or more curates to assist him in his duty, by the endowment of chapels of ease, or the institution of lectureships, the visitation of the sick in the parish is tolerably provided for;—still the want of a social organization remains the same. The parishioners, except in questions about rates, never act as a body, nor feel as a body. They have no part in keeping up any religious discipline; those amongst them who are qualified for instructing or exhorting their neighbours can do it only as individuals. The very church itself, closed during the greater part of the day, perhaps of the week, is opened only for the performance of one uniform service, never to be added to, never to be varied. Even the singing, where alone some degree of liberty has been left to the congregation, is in some dioceses brought down to the same uniformity, and nothing may be sung but the old and new versions of the Psalms of David. Thus the people are, as members of the Church, wholly passive;—the love of self-government, one of the best instincts in our nature, and one most opposite to the spirit of lawlessness, finds no place for its exercise; they neither govern themselves, nor is there any one else to govern them.

Division of Dioceses

In order to obtain an efficient and comprehensive Church system, the first thing necessary is to divide the actual dioceses. A government must be feeble where one bishop, as is the case in the diocese of Chester, has the nominal superintendence over a tract of country extending in length above a hundred miles, and over a population of nearly two millions of souls. Every large town should necessarily be the seat of a bishop, the bishopric thus created giving no seat in Parliament;—and the addition of such an element into the society of a commercial or manufacturing place, would be in itself a great advantage;—for as in small cathedral towns, the society is at present much too exclusively clerical, so in towns like Manchester and Birmingham, the influence of the clergy is too little; they are not in a condition to colour sufficiently the mass of a population whose employment is to make money. The present dioceses might then become provinces, or if it should be thought desirable to diminish the number of bishops in the House of Lords, the number retained might correspond to the number of provinces which it might be found convenient to constitute, so that metropolitan bishops alone should have seats in Parliament. And for the new bishoprics to be created, the deaneries throughout England would go a long way towards endowing them;—while in many cases nothing more would be required, than to change the name and office of the incumbent of the principal parish in the town; so that instead of being the minister of one church he should become the bishop of the diocese, the income of his office remaining the same as at present.

The several dioceses throughout England being thus rendered efficient in point of extent and population, it would be next required to organize their government. Episcopalians require that this should be *episcopal*; the Dissenters of almost every denomination would insist that it should not be *prelatical*. But it may be the first without being the last. Episcopacy may be regulated in two ways, so as to hinder it from being tyrannical; either by withdrawing almost every matter from its jurisdiction, according to the system now pursued in England, or by uniting and tempering it with an admixture of more popular authorities. But of these two expedients the first is equally destructive of the power of a bishop for good as for evil; the last would leave him at liberty to do good, but would merely restrain him from using his authority amiss. For instance, a bishop should be incapable of acting without his council, and this council should consist partly of lay members, and partly of clerical, to be appointed partly by himself, and partly by the ministers and lay elders of the several parishes in his diocese. A court would be thus formed, to which the maintenance of discipline might be safely entrusted, and ministers of scandalous life might be removed from their benefices without the tedious and ruinous process now imposed upon the bishop, if he is anxious to do his duty in such cases. Probably, too, it would be expedient to create something like a general assembly of the Church in each diocese, to meet at a certain time in the year, under the presidency of the bishop, and to enact such general regulations as might from time to time be needed. A meeting of this kind, even were its sittings ever so short, would be useful in the mere sensation that it would excite among the people; as it would present the Church to them in a form at once imposing and attractive, and would destroy that most mischievous notion which the present visitations rather tend to encourage—that the Church is synonymous with the clergy. Again, either this general assembly, or the bishop and his ordinary council, should have the power of increasing or reducing the number of church officers in any particular parish, and of settling the limits of their respective ministrations. Where one man's constant ministry is sufficient, the occasional assistance of more may yet be desirable; or if not a public, yet a domestic ministry, in addition to the public one, may be useful; that is, even in small country parishes there are often found men of serious character, who would be able and willing to preach to their neighbours, and who do preach, as things are at present, but with this evil, that they preach by their own authority, and are unavoidably led to feel themselves in opposition to the Establishment. Now, it is an obvious principle of every society, that men should not take its offices upon themselves without authority; and many persons who are now self-constituted teachers, would gladly obtain a sanction to their ministry, and would consent to put it under the regulation of the government of the Church, if such a recognition were rendered a thing easily obtainable. But in large towns, all the Christian ministers of every denomination actually employed in them are certainly not more than adequate to the wants of the population. That these could not be all maintained out of the funds of the present Establishment is manifest; it is possible that some might be; and it is also possible that some gratuitous assistance might be rendered by persons who, having another trade or profession, were not wholly dependent on the ministry for support. But as the *dissenting* ministers are actually maintained by voluntary contributions, so the *assistant* ministers of a more comprehensive system, whether their opinions were in exact agreement with the present articles or not, would be easily, and I believe most cheerfully maintained by Easter offerings, levied upon all the members of the Church, and divided according to the qualifications and labours of the respective ministers. And as these would all be equally ministers of the National Church, they would have their share in the election of the clerical members of the bishop's council, and would be effectually secured against any lurking spirit of sectarian hostility which might be supposed to survive the overthrow of the present sectarian system.

Appointments

But it may be said that a difficulty would arise as to the manner in which these ministers should be appointed; their election by their congregations being as odious to one class of persons, as it is dear to another. It seems to me desirable that a national Church should comprehend in itself many various ways of appointment; and that whilst the patronage of the existing benefices should on no account be disturbed, whether it be vested in the crown, or in corporate bodies, or in private individuals; yet, that where there is no endowment, and the minister is paid by a general contribution, the principle of election may fitly be allowed. But the actual abuses of all patronage, whether individual or popular, might easily be obviated by certain general regulations. It is a great evil, that a worthless individual, whether nominated by a private patron, or chosen by a misguided majority, should immediately and without further question enter upon his ministry. All patronage should be strictly recommendatory, and no more: the patron or electors should send the object of their choice to the bishop and his council, or, if it were thought fit, to another distinct tribunal, appointed by them; and here his qualifications should undergo a most rigid scrutiny. If he were rejected, the patron should recommend another candidate; but never should his recommendation, or the election of the inhabitants, be deemed equivalent to an actual appointment. And even when confirmed by the Church authorities, it should still be, in the first instance, only provisional, for one year; that during that time he might be tried in actual service, and if any just ground of objection existed against him, which might well happen without supposing any such misconduct as should warrant his removal from an office conferred for life, the appointment might be either wholly cancelled, according to the nature of the case, or the term of probation extended to a longer period.

In suggesting that the qualifications of every person recommended to a benefice should be rigorously scrutinized, I am far from meaning that he should be subjected to an examination. Examinations can only be fitly applied to young men, and their proper place is previous to ordination, not when a man, after having been ordained, is to be appointed to some particular cure. Yet, in a matter of such importance, every security is needed; and more is required than the present system of testimonials, not only from their proved insufficiency, but because the people should have a more direct check than they have at present on the nomination of their ministers. It should be the duty of the parish authorities, both lay and clerical, to report fully to the bishop's council, all that they can collect as to the character and general fitness of the person recommended by the patron. For instance, a senior fellow of a college, however irreproachable in his character, may, from his inactive and retired habits, be an unfit person to be appointed minister of a populous parish in a large town. It would be the duty of the parish authorities to represent this to the bishop's council; and in some cases the objection might be so strong, owing to local circumstances, as to render it proper to reject the person proposed altogether. But in every case it would be desirable that the appointment should, in the first instance, be only temporary, that it might be seen how the individual could accommodate himself to a life so different from his past one, whether his previous habits were or were not alterable. And we may be sure that the working of every system will be so much more indulgent than the theory, that we never need fear an excess of strictness; do what we will, considerations of good-nature and kindness to an individual, will always prevail in the long-run over the sense of public duty.

Summary of Administrative Reform

The Church government then would be made more efficient, and at the same time, more popular than it is at present; 1st. By reducing the size of the dioceses: 2nd. By giving the bishop a council consisting of lay members and of clerical, and partly elected by the officers of the respective parishes; which officers should themselves also be lay and clerical, and for the most part elected directly by the inhabitants: 3rd. By the institution of diocesan general assemblies: 4th. By admitting into the Establishment, persons of a class much too poor to support the expense of an university education; but who may be exceedingly useful as ministers, and who do preach at present, but under circumstances which make them necessarily hostile to the National Church, and leave them utterly at liberty to follow their own caprices: 5th. By allowing in many cases the election of ministers, and by giving to the inhabitants of the parish in every case, a greater check over their appointment than they at present enjoy: and 6th. By constituting Church officers in every parish, lay as well clerical, who should share with the principal minister in its superintendence; and thus effect generally that good, which in London and elsewhere is now being attempted by individual zeal, in the establishment of district visiting societies. Whilst by rendering the Articles far more comprehensive than at present, according to what was said in the earlier part of this sketch, those who are now Dissenting ministers might at once become ministers of the Establishment, and as such, would of course have their share in its government.

Bishops in Church and State

It will be observed, that the whole of this scheme supposes an episcopal government, and requires that all ministers should receive episcopal ordination. The Establishment is entitled surely to this concession from the Dissenters, especially when Episcopacy will have been divested of all those points against which their objections have been particularly levelled. Besides, there are many members of the Establishment who believe Episcopacy not expedient only, but absolutely essential to a Christian Church: and their scruples are entitled to quite as much respect as those of the Dissenters. And when experience has shown that Episcopalians will be satisfied if the mere name of a bishop is preserved—for nothing can be more different in all essential points, than our Episcopacy and that of the primitive Church—and as this name is recommended not only by its ancient and almost universal use throughout Christendom, but by its familiarity to ourselves, and its long existence in our own constitution, there seems every reason why it should be retained,—and why those who may have objected to a prelate lording it over Christ's Church with absolute authority, may readily acknowledge the limited authority of a bishop, the president of his council of elders, supreme in rank, but controlled effectually in power.

This, perhaps, may be the fittest place to notice the clamour in which the Dissenters have blindly joined the unbelievers, against the bishops holding seats in the House of Lords. Never was there a question on which fanaticism and narrow-mindedness have so completely played into the hands of wickedness. The very notion of the House of Lords, is that of an assembly embracing the highest portions of the most eminent professions or classes of society. Accordingly, it contains, speaking generally, the most considerable of the landed proprietors of the kingdom, the most distinguished individuals in the army and navy; and in like manner a certain number of the heads of the clerical profession, and of the law. It is not that the Lord Chancellor and the Bishops are the representatives of their respective professions, in the sense of being placed in Parliament to look after their particular interests; nor is it at all for the sake of the clergy or the lawyers that they sit in the House of Peers, but for the sake of the nation; that the highest national council may have the benefit of their peculiar knowledge, and peculiar views of life. Now it is manifest, that all of what are called the liberal professions, exercise a certain influence over the minds of those who follow them both for good and for evil;—for evil, so far as they lead to exclusiveness—for good, inasmuch as they foster particular faculties of the mind, and give an especial power of appreciating and enforcing one class of important truths. As then, in an assembly consisting of men of one profession only, the evil influence becomes predominant and pedantry and narrow-mindedness are sure to be its characteristics; so when men of different professions are mixed, the evil of a professional spirit is neutralized, while its advantages remain in full force; and in proportion to the greater number of professions thus brought together in one assembly, will be the universality of its tone, and at the same time the soundness of its particular resolutions.

Lord Henley, therefore, labours under a double error when he supposes that the revival of any sort of ecclesiastical synod or convocation could be a substitute for the sitting of the bishops in Parliament, and when he talks of allowing the bishops to vote only on such questions as concern the *Church.* A synod or convocation might look as effectually after the interests of the clergy; but how would it compensate for the removal of one important element from the constitution of our highest national assembly? And again, when he speaks of questions which concern the Church, he means questions about the duties and payment of the clergy—an important part certainly of Church questions—but by no means the most important, still less the only ones. According to this narrow view of the meaning of the word Church, thc bishops may vote upon a curate's salary bill, or a church building act; but the weightier matters of the law, judgment, mercy, and truth, are questions which affect the Church no more than the Royal Society. In other words, it concerns not the Church whether its members are involved in the guilt and misery of an unnecessary war,—whether their laws are regardless of human life, and multiply temptations to crime;—whether, in short, their institutions and form of society are favourable to their moral advancement, or tend, on the contrary, to debase and to harden them.

But, says Lord Henley, the Divine Founder of the Church has declared that his kingdom was not of this world, and he "refused to give sentence in a criminal cause of adultery, and in a civil one of dividing an inheritance," p. 49. It might make Lord Henley and other good men a little suspicious of the applicability of our Lord's words to the present question, if they would remember how favourite a text they are with men who scarcely know any single declaration of our Lord's besides this, and who clearly and almost avowedly fear nothing so much as that the world should really become his kingdom. But first of all, if Christ's kingdom be not of this world, in the only sense which applies to the present question, if his Church may have nothing to do with making and repealing laws, approving of peace and war, imposing taxes, and other such matters, it follows distinctly, not that every clergyman, but that every Christian, should instantly be excluded from the Throne, from Parliament, and from every public office whatever, whether civil or military. We should require from members of Parliament no declarations against transubstantiation,—but simply a protestation that they did not belong to the kingdom of Christ, but were, and would remain so, faithful subjects of the kingdom of the world, and bound to do the god of this world true and undivided service. It is perfectly inconceivable how a man like Lord Henley can go on, page after page, using the word "Church" to signify the clergy, when he must know it is never used so in the New Testament; and that every passage which he quotes against mixing in secular affairs, applies exactly as much to the Lord Chancellor and the Commander-in-Chief, if they are Christians, as to the Archbishop of Canterbury.

Lord Henley objects to "the example of such Jewish precedents as Eli and Ezra", p. 49. By what strange perversity does it happen, that the party to which Lord Henley seems to belong, should refuse to acknowledge the authority of Old Testament precedents, in the very case where they are really applicable, and yet should be for ever appealing to them where they are not applicable at all? Eli and Ezra are in this matter far more to the purpose than Paul, or Peter, or John; because, in their days, as in ours, the kingdom of God was a kingdom of the world also; whereas, in the days of the apostles it was not so. It is absolutely ridiculous in a country where Christianity is said to be the law of the land,

—where all our institutions acknowledge it, and our kings are actually anointed before the altar,—to quote as applicable the state of the Christians of the first century, whose religion necessarily drew them away from all public duties, because heathenism and heathen principles were so mixed up with all the institutions of Rome, that every public office involved some compliance with them.

It is again a most groundless superstition, and one which at once occasioned and has been increased by the mischievous confusion of the Christian ministry with a *priesthood,* that any thing can be lawful for a Christian layman which is unlawful for a Christian minister. As the ministers are in a manner picked out from the whole Christian body, it may be within possibility to exact from them a higher standard of practice than can be enforced generally; but this is no more than saying, "what *all ought to be,* we will take care that *some* at least *shall be.*" If any one looks at the qualifications required by St. Paul in the ministers of the Church (1 Tim. iii. 1-10. Titus i. 6-9), he will find amongst them no esoteric purity of life or fulness of knowledge; but the virtues of a good man, a good public officer, and a good Christian;—the virtues which become, and are to be expected of, every one invested with authority in the Church of God, whether his peculiar ministry be on the seat of justice, or at the altar, or in the general government of the whole society.

But because these virtues are now become rare, because there may be found in the other ministries of the Church, men who do not acknowledge their obligation, therefore it is the more important that they who are called ministers in a peculiar sense, the ministers at the altar, should be put forward in situations where they can most loudly and most efficiently enforce them. And this is the great reason why the clergy ought to sit in both houses of Parliament, and why the enemies of Christianity, who well understand the interests of *their* Master, would gladly exclude them from both. It is because they are not priests, but Christians; because they hold and know no esoteric doctrine; because they are required to practise no virtue beyond the rest of their brethren, but yet because their profession obliges them to know what Christianity is, and public opinion, to take the lowest ground, hinders them from utterly casting it off in their practice, that therefore they are wanted in the national assembly of a professedly Christian nation. What we ought to calculate on in every member of the legislature—namely, that he should speak and act on Christian principles—we are obliged now to look for from those who are bound to be Christians by a double profession, by their ordination as well as their baptism. In proportion to the proved insufficiency of one of these securities singly, is the need of applying to the combined strength of both.

But what if the salt has lost its savour; if in point of fact the bishops have not thus diffused the influence of Christianity through the House of Lords: whose has been the fault, and what is its remedy? Was not the fault theirs, who for so many years, I may almost say so many generations, made the appointment of a bishop a mere matter of patronage; or, at the best, the reward of ability and knowledge displayed on some mere abstract question of theology? Was not, and is not, the fault theirs, who, some in fraud and others in simplicity, adopting Lord Henley's confusion about the word Church, would confine the bishops to speaking on merely professional subjects, and would accuse them of meddling with secular matters, if they were to endeavour to christianize the laws or the measures of the government? Is not the fault above all, theirs, who, retaining the system of translation for the sake of their own patronage, place the bishops in a situation of certain suspicion, and of unfair temptation? And is it not the most obvious remedy to do away at once and entirely with the system of translations, and thus to make the bishops the most independent of any men in the House of Lords. For a lay lord, if he is an able and active man, may hope to rise to power by displacing an existing ministry, or by supporting them; a bishop, if translations were at an end, would have nothing to hope for from courtliness or from faction: he could gain nothing by basely voting for the government,—nothing by ambitiously and unfairly molesting them.

This digression, if such it can be called, has somewhat interrupted the main divisions of my argument; but it is naturally connected with the question of Church government, and no part of the whole subject has been so mistakenly and so mischievously handled.

Unity of Practice

I now return to the third division of my inquiry: whether it be not possible to unite in one Church great varieties of ritual,—in other words, whether uniformity of worship has been wisely made the object of our ecclesiastical legislation.

Liturgy

The friends of the Established Church justly extol the substantial excellence and beauty of the liturgy. It can indeed hardly be praised too highly as the solemn service of the Church, embodying one of the best representations of the feelings and language of a true Christian, in his confessions, his thanksgivings, and his prayers. But as, while we reverence the Bible above all other books, we yet should never think of studying it to the exclusion of all others, so, and much more, may we say of the liturgy, that, even allowing it to be the best conceivable religious service in itself, still it ought not to be the only one. The liturgy of the Church of England, with some few alterations, which I need not here specify, should be used once on every Sunday and every great Christian holiday throughout the year, in every parish church in England. But I doubt whether there are not many, even amongst its most sincere admirers, who, in a second service on the same day, would be glad of some variety,—still more who would wish to vary the service according to the time and circumstances, when the church was opened on week days. Indeed, I hardly know a more painful sight than the uninterrupted loneliness in which our churches are so often left from one Sunday to another. The very communion table and pulpit are dismantled of their coverings and cushions; the windows are closed; the doors fast locked, as is a Protestant church, except on a Sunday, were like the Pelasgicum at Athens, "best when unfrequented."[a] Now this has arisen partly, no doubt, from other causes; but the necessity of reading the Liturgy, and nothing but the Liturgy, both at morning and evening prayer, is an invincible obstacle to the opening of the churches generally with any effect, except on a Sunday. It is doubtful whether our arrangement of our time, and the universal pressure of business, would allow of the attendance of a large congregation at church on week days, under any circumstances; but it is certain, that in order to overcome these disadvantages, something more attractive is needed than the mere uniform reading of the same prayers, and going through the same forms day after day, both in the morning and the evening. Nor should I think it an evil, but a great good, that different services should be performed at different times of the day and week, within the walls of the same church. Not only do the various tastes and degrees of knowledge amongst men require varieties in the form of their religious services; but the very same men are not always in the mood for the same things: there are times when we should feel most in unison with the deep solemnity of the Liturgy; there are times also, when we should better enjoy a freer and more social service; and for the sake of the greater familiarity, should pardon some insipidity and some extravagance. And he who condemns

[a] *Τὸ Πελασγικὸν ἀργὸν ἄμεινον.*—Thucyd. II, 17.

this feeling, does but lose his labour, and can but ill appreciate one great attribute of God's works,—their endless variety. Our sight, our hearing, and our taste, are furnished with subjects of gratification, not of one kind only, but of millions; the morning song of the lark is not the same with the evening song of the nightingale: the scenery which we most enjoy in the full brightness of a summer day, is not that which best harmonizes with the solemnity of an autumn evening.

Now, considering that some persons would like nothing but the Liturgy, that others, on the contrary, can endure no prayers but such as are extemporaneous,—that many more have a preference for one practice or the other, but not so as to wish to be confined to the exclusive use of it, there seems to be no reason why the National Church should not enjoy a sufficient variety in its ritual, to satisfy the opinions and feelings of all. In a parish where there was but one minister, he might read the Liturgy on Sunday mornings, while on Sunday evenings, and on week days, he might vary the service according to his discretion and the circumstances of the case. But where there were several ministers, as there would be wherever there are now ministers of different denominations, the church might be kept open nearly the whole of the Sunday, and we may hope, during some part at least of every week day;—the different services being fixed at different hours, and performed by different ministers. And he judges untruly of human nature, who does not see that the peculiarities which men now cling to and even exaggerate, as the badge and mark of their own sect, would then soon sink into their proper insignificance when nothing was to be gained by dwelling on them. Good men, feeling that they might express their opinions freely, and that their silence could not be misconstrued into fear or insincerity, would gladly listen to their better nature, which would teach them how much they had in common with one another, and how infinitely their points of agreement surpassed in importance their points of difference. And instead of an unseemly scene of one minister preaching against another, we should probably have an earnest union in great matters, and a manly and delicate forbearance as to points of controversy, such as would indeed become the disciples of Him who is in equal perfection the God of truth and the God of love.

Place of Worship

It may appear to some a point of small importance, but I believe that it would go a long way towards producing a kindly and united feeling amongst all the inhabitants of the parish, that the parish church should, if possible, be the only place of public worship; and that the different services required, should rather be performed at different times in the same spot than at the same time in different places. In this respect, the spirit of the Mosaic law may be most usefully followed, which forbade the multiplication of temples and altars, but fixed on one spot to become endeared and hallowed to the whole people as the scene of their common worship. Besides the parish church has a sacredness which no other place of worship can boast of, in its antiquity, and in its standing amidst the graves of so many generations of our fathers. It is painful to think that any portion of the people should have ever broken their connexion with it; it would be equally delightful to see them again assembled within its walls, without any base compromise of opinion on either side, but because we had learned a better wisdom than to deprive it of its just claim to the affections of all our countrymen, or to exclude any portion of our countrymen from the happiness of loving it as it deserves. Nor is it a light thing in the judgments of those who understand the ennobling effects of a quick perception of what is beautiful and venerable, that some of the most perfect specimens of architecture in existence should no longer be connected, in any man's mind, with the bitterness of sectarian hostility; that none should be forced to associate, with their most solemn and dearest recollections, such utter coarseness and deformity as characterize the great proportion of the Dissenting chapels throughout England.

The appointment of various services in the same church, would not only be desirable in itself, but would also obviate the necessity of altering our own Liturgy, in order to enable the Dissenters to join in it; for even if we could overcome their objections to any Liturgy whatever as such, still the differences of mere taste between different classes of people are so great, as to render it impossible to contrive any one service such as should be satisfactory to one party without a needful sacrifice of what is a great source of pleasure to the other. For instance, some of the Dissenters object to an organ, and to all but the simplest kinds of church music: yet it would be very unreasonable to pull down our organs, and to banish our anthems, and all the magnificence of our cathedral service, without considering that numerous class who feel as much delighted and edified by these things as others are offended at them. On the other hand, it is quite as unreasonable, and much more unchristian, to make a difference of taste a reason for continuing divisions in the Church of God. There is no reason why all should not be gratified without quarrelling with each other; why the organ should not sound at the morning service, and be silent in the evening: why the same roof which had rung at one part of the day with the rich music of a regular choir, should not at another resound with the simpler but not less impressive singing of a mixed congregation.

Other Reforms Required

Such as it seems to me, is the reform really needed;—to make the Church truly and effectually the "Church of

England". Many points, about which there is the loudest clamour, I have passed over without notice;—partly, because for these there have been remedies proposed by other writers,—and partly, because I hold them to be utterly subordinate grievances when compared to the monstrous evil of sectarianism. The evil of pluralities is like that of sinecures and unmerited pensions in the state;—it should be removed, because it is unseemly and discreditable; but it is only folly or bad faith which would rank it amongst the most serious practical mischiefs of our ecclesiastical system. The inequality of ranks and emoluments in the Church, like that existing also in the whole frame of our society, is probably excessive; but is a far less evil than the platform of equality to which some would reduce it. Even non-residence itself,—by which I mean the non-residence of any minister of the Establishment, whether incumbent or curate, happens accidentally to be only of inferior importance, because it generally exists in country parishes, where the amount of population is small. Destroy it altogether, and the efficiency of the Church would be increased in a scarcely perceptible degree; for its great inefficiency as a national establishment arises from other causes,—from the enormous population of the towns, where the minister of the parish *is* generally resident, but utterly incapable of doing the work which he is nominally set to perform,—and from the other large masses of population, to whom the ministers of the Establishment are nothing, whether resident or not, because they have separated themselves from the national communion. With regard to the cry about the bishops, translation is certainly indefensible,—and its utter extinction highly needful: some means also should be taken to increase the revenue of the poorer bishoprics; and for this object something probably might well be spared from the revenue of those that are richest. But the sitting of the bishops in Parliament is a great national good; and a multiplication of their number, with a remodelling of their power, so as to give the Church a real episcopal government, is the reform of their order most needed and most effectual.

Nor have I said a word on the great question of Tithes, because I have reason to believe that that question is in other and far abler hands. All acknowledge the odiousness of the present manner of payment;—but the problem hitherto has been, how to provide for it an adequate substitute (6).

3

CONCLUSION

Reform of Existing Establishment not Enough

But suppose Tithes to be commuted,—the revenues of the Clergy equalized,—residence universally enforced,—and pluralities done away with, the efficiency of the Establishment, as a great social engine of intellectual, moral, and religious good, will still be incomplete,—and for this very reason its stability will be precarious. There will still remain that vast mass of the dissenting and of the godless population, who, not sharing in its benefits, will labour to effect its destruction. These two parties are leagued together; and unless their league can be dissolved, the long continuance of a national Church in this country is a thing impossible. The cry which is destroying the Protestant Establishment in Ireland is already beginning to be echoed here: the Dissenters repeat the complaint of the Catholics, —"Why should we be obliged to contribute towards the maintenance of a Church which is not ours?" All the inherent evils of our detestable sectarian system will presently be brought to light, and will derange the very frame of society. Church rates have been already resisted;—that is to say, the noblest and most useful of all our public buildings will be suffered to go to ruin, or to be maintained by private munificence. Marriage, the most important of all social ordinances, will be made a private ceremony;—for such must be the character of a rite performed without the intervention of any public officer; whether that officer be a magistrate or a clergyman, may be a question of comparative indifference; for in either case society sanctions, and in a manner presides at the celebration of its holiest contract; but a Dissenting minister is a mere private individual, or rather an alien from the national society, to whose acts society lends no authority. The registration of births, marriages, and deaths, a thing essentially of national concern, and to be placed under the control of public officers, is already claimed by the Dissenters as a right to be enjoyed by their own communities separately. Our universities, the great seats of public education, are in danger of becoming odious, because they are practically closed against so large a portion of the community;—while the evils of Dissenting colleges, pledged by their very name to narrow-mindedness, will continue to multiply. The end of all this will be, what the godless party are earnestly labouring to effect, the dissolution of the Establishment altogether;—that is, in other words, the public renouncing of our allegiance to God; for without an Establishment, although it may happen that the majority of Englishmen may still be Christians, yet England will not be a Christian nation;—its government will be no Christian government;—we shall be wholly a kingdom of the world, and ruled according to none but worldly principles. In such a state the establishment of paganism would be an absolute blessing; any thing would be better than a national society, formed for no higher than physical ends;—to enable men to eat, drink, and live luxuriously;—acknowledging no power greater than its own, and by consequence, no law higher than its own municipal enactments. Let a few generations pass over in such a state, and the missionary, who should preach the worship of Ceres, or set up an oracle of Apollo, or teach the people to kindle the eternal fire of Vesta on the common altar hearth of their country, would be to that degraded society as life from the dead.

I cannot resist the pleasure of copying here the beautiful

lines in which Mr. Wordsworth sympathizes so entirely with the feeling expressed in the text:

"The world is too much with us; late and soon,
Getting and spending, we lay waste our powers;
Little we see in nature that is ours;
We have given our hearts away, a sordid boon!
This sea, that bears her bosom to the moon;
The winds, that will be howling at all hours,
And are up-gathered now like sleeping flowers;
For this, for every thing, we are out of tune;
It moves us not. Great God! I'd rather be
A pagan suckled in a creed outworn;
So might I, standing on this pleasant lea,
Have glimpses that would make me less forlorn;
Have a sight of Proteus rising from the sea,
Or hear old Triton blow his wreathed horn" (7).

But we are told to look at America; the United States have no national religion; but yet we are assured that they are as religious a people as ourselves (8). When a man of science hears a fact asserted in direct contradiction to the known laws of nature, he cannot but suspect some misrepresentation or confusion in the statement. To assert that the irregular efforts of individual zeal and courage will oppose an invading enemy as effectually as a good regular army, would be little better than insanity; and yet it may be true, that in the last war the Spanish guerillas did more service to their country than the Spanish regular armies. We know, however, that the guerillas did not, and could not deliver Spain; it was an efficient regular army which achieved that work. So, if it could be shown that under any circumstances Christianity was flourishing as much without an Establishment as with one, it would merely prove that the particular Establishment in question was in a state of deplorable corruption, as it had so completely forfeited its inherent advantages. But in the alleged instance of the

United States, we forget that "America" is, in the first place, a very vague word, and that in those parts of the union in which religion is in the healthiest state, there is what is almost equivalent to an Establishment; that is, every man is obliged to contribute to a fund for religious instruction, but he has his choice as to the particular sect to which his quota is to be paid. Again, the Episcopal Church in New York is an endowed church; it still possesses the lands assigned to it by the British government, previously to the revolution. It may well be then that in New York, and in some of the New England states, the people may be more religious than in the great towns of England; but this concludes in favour of an Establishment, not against one; because there is an Establishment, or what amounts to nearly the same thing, in these parts of the United States, whereas there is virtually none in our great towns; so utterly inadequate is the supply of ministers to the demands of the ever-growing population. But if it be asserted, that in the southern and western states, society is in as healthy a state morally and religiously as in those parts of England where the Church is enabled to be efficient, then I should deny the fact altogether. With all the advantages enjoyed by America, as to the physical condition of her people, with her prodigious extent of available land, and her as yet comparatively scanty population, rendering the temptation to offences against property far less than it can be in an old and fully peopled country; still the world has as yet produced no instance of society advancing under a less promising aspect, intellectual, moral, and religious, than in the new states and territories of the American union.

But if we with our overflowing population and narrow limits were wilfully to plunge ourselves into the moral and religious state of southern and western America, the evils of their condition would be multiplied a thousand-fold here. Crowded together as we are, we cannot afford to be disorderly; it is well if, with all the aid of the most powerful and the purest institutions, we can organize and keep from taint the unwieldly masses of our population. And as the best of all institutions, I am anxious to secure a truly national Church, which, uniting within itself all Christians who deserve the name, except perhaps the mere handful of the Quakers and Roman Catholics, would leave without its pale nothing but voluntary or involuntary godlessness. We should hear no complaints then of the burden of supporting a Church to which men do not belong. Such language in a Dissenter's mouth is forcible; but who would heed it from a man who belonged to no church, who paid no minister of his own,—but hating God altogether, was consistently averse to contributing towards his service? Truly we may wait a long time before we shall find the thieves of a country willing to pay for the building of gaols, or the maintenance of an efficient police.

Agents of Reform

But, it may be said, admitting the soundness of the principles put forward in these pages, that the National Church should be rendered thoroughly comprehensive in doctrine, in government, and in ritual, by what power are they to be carried into effect? To whose hands, in particular, should be committed the delicate task of remodelling the Articles, a measure obviously essential to the proposed comprehension, yet presenting the greatest practical difficulty? It seems to me, that this is a question more properly to be answered by the Government, than by an individual; only, I may be allowed to express an earnest hope, that if ever an union with Dissenters be attempted, and it should thus become necessary to alter our present terms of communion, the determining on the alterations to be made should never be committed to a convocation, or to any commission consisting of clergymen alone. It is the more needful to express this opinion strongly, because Lord Henley, while himself looking forward to an extension of the pale of the Church, declares that this is "exclusively a theological and ecclesiastical duty, and that no layman can take, or should desire to take, any part in the execution of it". So completely does his confused notion of what is meant by the Church pervade and vitiate every part of his work. Well has Mr. Hull (9) observed, with reference to this notion, that "it breathes too little sense of Protestant responsibility". "We cannot be justified," he adds, "in neglecting the public service of our Creator, our Redeemer, and our Sanctifier; and must, therefore, at our own peril, look well to the method in which that public service is conducted and maintained." Laymen have no right to shift from their own shoulders an important part of Christian responsibility; and as no educated layman individually is justified in taking his own faith upon trust from a clergyman, so neither are the laity, as a body, warranted in taking the national faith in the same way. If ever it should be thought right to appoint commissioners to revise the Articles, it is of paramount importance, in order to save the plan from utter failure, that a sufficient number of laymen, distinguished for their piety and enlarged views, should be added to the ecclesiastical members of the commission. Professional learning, if not sufficiently tempered with the straight-forward views of a plain and sensible piety, would be absolutely mischievous; as it would lead men to retain the language of former controversies, where it is most important, both for the sake of truth and charity, that the statement should be general, and should adopt no technical terms whatever in declaring doctrines, beyond such as may be used in the Scriptures themselves.

As for the proposed constitution of the government and ritual[a] of the Church, this would be naturally and in the

[a] By "ritual" I do not mean to include the alterations to be made in the Liturgy, and which would be the proper business of the commission appointed to revise the Articles; but only the repealing

first place the subject of legislative enactment; nor would it be more difficult to draw up the necessary details in this case, than it was found to be in the case of the Reform Bill. Care and attention would of course be requisite; and information on many points must be sought from persons locally or professionally qualified to furnish it; but there is nothing in the subject-matter itself which can render the previous report of any other authority necessary, before the question is submitted by the king's Government to the consideration and decision of Parliament.

In venturing even to suggest so great a change in the constitution of our Church, I may probably expose myself to a variety of imputations. Above all, whoever pleads in favour of a wide extension of the terms of communion, is immediately apt to be accused of latitudinarianism, or as it is now called, of liberalism. Such a charge in the mouths of men at once low principled and ignorant, is of no importance whatever; neither should I regard it if it proceeded from the violent fanatical party, to whom truth must ever remain unknown, as it is unsought after. But in the Church of England even bigotry often wears a softer and a nobler aspect; and there are men at once pious, high minded, intelligent, and full of all kindly feelings, whose intensive love for the forms of the Church, fostered as it has been by all the best associations of their pure and holy lives, has absolutely engrossed their whole nature; they have neither eyes to see of themselves any defect in the Liturgy or Articles, nor ears to hear of such when alleged by others. It can be no ordinary church to have inspired such a devoted adoration in such men;—nor are they ordinary men over whom the sense of high moral beauty has obtained so complete a mastery. They will not, I fear, be willing to believe how deeply painful it is to my mind, to

those laws which permit nothing but the Liturgy to be read in the Church, and enjoin that it shall be read itself both at Morning and Evening Prayer.

know that I am regarded by them as an adversary; still more to feel that I am associated in their judgments with principles and with a party which I abhor as deeply as they do. But while I know the devotedness of their admiration for the Church of England, as it is now constituted, I cannot but wish that they would regard those thousands and ten thousands of their countrymen, who are excluded from its benefit; that they would consider the wrong done to our common country by these unnatural divisions amongst her children. *The Church of Christ* is indeed far beyond all human ties; but of all human ties, that to our country is the highest and most sacred: and *England,* to a true Englishman, ought to be dearer than the peculiar forms of *the Church of England.*

For the sake, then, of our country, and to save her from the greatest possible evils,—from evils far worse than any loss of territory, or decline of trade,—from the sure moral and intellectual degradation which will accompany the unchristianizing of the nation, that is, the destroying of its national religious establishment, is it too much to ask of good men, that they should consent to unite themselves with other good men, without requiring them to subscribe to their own opinions, or to conform to their own ceremonies? They are not asked to surrender or compromise the smallest portion of their own faith, but simply to forbear imposing it upon their neighbours. They are not called upon to give up their own forms of worship, but to allow the addition of others; not for themselves to join in it, if they do not like to do so, but simply to be celebrated in the same church, and by ministers, whom they shall acknowledge to be their brethren, and members no less than themselves of the National Establishment. The alterations which should be made in their own Liturgy should be such as, to use Bishop Burnet's (10) words, "are in themselves desirable, though there were not a Dissenter in the nation"; alterations not to change its character, but to perfect it.

Answers to Objections

That Arnold's Proposals are Latitudinarian

"But it is latitudinarian not to lay a greater stress on the necessity of believing the truth, and to allow by public authority, and sanction by our own co-operation, the teaching of error." I will not yield to any man in the strength of my conviction of truth and error; nor in the wish that the propagation of error could be prevented. But how is it possible to effect this? How many of the sermons and other writings of our best divines contain more or less of error, of foolish arguments, of false premises, of countervailing truths unknown or neglected, so that even the truth on the other side, being stated alone, becomes virtually no better than falsehood! How many passages of Scripture are misinterpreted in every translation and in every commentary! But are we to refuse to co-operate with our neighbour because of these errors; or shall our own love of truth be impeached because of our union with him? Every one knows, that it is a question of degree and detail; but with a discipline watching over a man's practice, and with a sincere acknowledgment of the authority of the New Testament, although much and serious error may yet be maintained and propagated, yet it is better even to suffer this, than by insisting on too great an agreement, necessarily to reduce our numbers, and bring upon our country the fearful risk of losing the establishment of Christianity altogether.

Men are alarmed by the examples of Germany and Geneva. But what do they prove? The latter proves admirably the mischiefs of an over-strict creed; and ultra-Calvinism was likely to lead to ultra-Socinianism, with the change of times in other respects. But at this moment the mischief in Geneva consists in the enforcement of the exclusive principle, not in its abandonment: the Church is now exclusively Arian or Socinian, as it was once exclusively Calvinistic; and Trinitarian ministers are not allowed to teach to their congregations the great and peculiar doctrines of Christianity. And with regard to the Germans; had the Protestant Churches there retained ever so exclusively a body of articles, yet the strong tendency of the national character would probably have led to the same result: with no other difference than the addition of the evil of hypocrisy to that of ultra-rationalism. For let any man observe the German literature in other branches besides theology; and he will see the same spirit of restless inquiry everywhere pervading it. Nor is it confined in theology to the German Protestants; the Catholics are not exempt from it; only there, from the nature of their Church, it is displayed less sincerely, and therefore, I think, much more painfully. As an instance of this covert rationalism, I should name a book which has been translated into English, and has had some circulation in this country, "Hug's Introduction to the Study of the New Testament" (11).

For us, on the other hand, critical and metaphysical questions have but small attractions; we have little to fear from the evil of indulging in them to excess. Unbelief, with us, is mostly the result of moral and political causes; to check which, nothing would be so efficient as a well-organized and comprehensive National Church, acting unitedly and popularly, and with adequate means, upon the whole mass of our population. The widest conceivable difference of opinion between the ministers of such a Church would be a trifling evil compared with the good of their systematic union of action.

That Arnold's Proposals are Impracticable

Lastly, if it be said that the changes proposed are too great,—that the scheme is visionary and impracticable; I answer, that the changes proposed are great, because the danger threatening us is enormous; and that although the scheme very probably will be impracticable, because men will persist in believing it to be so without trial, yet that it remains to be shown that it is impracticable in itself. But if the Reform of the Church be impracticable, its destruction unhappily is not so, and *that* its enemies know full well. It may be that a patchwork reform will be deemed safer, as assuredly it is easier; it may be, too, that after such a reform has been effected, and has left the great evils of the Church just where it found them, so that its final destruction shall be no less sure, the blame of its destruction will be laid by some on the principle of reform, and we shall be told that had no pretended improvements been attempted in it, it would have stood for ever. So it is, that no man is ever allowed to have died from the violence of his disease; but from the presumption of his physician, whose remedies, tried at the eleventh hour, he was too weak to bear. If I have seemed to speak confidently, it is not that I forget the usual course of human affairs; abuses and inefficient institutions obstinately retained, and then at last, blindly and furiously destroyed. Yet, when interests of such surpassing value are at stake, it may be allowable to hope even against hope; to suppress no plan which we conscientiously believe essential to our country's welfare, even though no other result should follow than that we should be ridiculed as theoretical, or condemned as presumptuous.

POSTSCRIPT

Answers to Objections

Since the first publication of this pamphlet I have heard and read a great many objections against its principles and details. But a very recent work on Church Reform, by the Rev. C. Dickinson, Domestic Chaplain to the Archbishop of Dublin (12), has particularly determined me to add some explanation and defence of what I have written; for Mr. Dickinson's objections are levelled against that part of my pamphlet which rests on principles most commonly misunderstood; and the tone of his remarks is at the same time so friendly, that it is impossible for any acrimonious feelings to mingle with my re-statement of my argument.

The substance of what I endeavoured to show was this, —that a Church Establishment is one of the greatest national blessings; that its benefits have been lessened, and are now in danger of being forfeited altogether, by its being based on too narrow a foundation, and being not so much the Church of England, as of a certain part only of the people of England; and that in order at once to secure it from destruction, and to increase its efficiency as an instrument of national good, it should be made more comprehensive in its doctrines, its constitution, and its ritual.

The first proposition, namely, that a Church Establishment is a great national blessing, is disputed sufficiently in many quarters, but not in those from which most of the objections to my pamphlet have proceeded. Nor have I met with any attempt to disprove the most important part of my second proposition,—that is, the actual jeopardy in which the Establishment as at present constituted is placed, from the strength of the several parties who are working together to effect its overthrow. And yet this is the main ground on which I urge the necessity of so extensive a reform: for although it might be an improvement upon our present system under any circumstances, yet if the Church, as it now is, were in no danger, I am quite ready to allow that it would be unwise to risk, supposing the proposed change to be a risk, the great benefits which the country even now derives from it, merely in the hope of making them greater.

On Comprehension

But against my third proposition, that the Establishment should be made more comprehensive, a surprising outcry has been raised. Some, as I expected, have ridiculed it as impracticable, while others have protested against it as latitudinarian[a] and contrary to the truth of Christ's Gospel; and the whole argument connected with it has been assailed on various grounds, and with various degrees of understanding, of good feeling, and of knowledge.

"The proposed comprehension is impracticable." It may possibly be so, and it is not only possible, but very likely, that I may have spoken too sanguinely of its *immediate* practicability in its full extent. I have supposed it impossible to include at present the Roman Catholics, the Quakers, and the Unitarians: it may be, that other bodies of Dissenters whom we might be willing to admit, would themselves object to the union, and would prefer their present independence, especially if they can succeed in obtaining relief from what they consider the burdens of their actual condition. Undoubtedly if they do obtain this

[a] "A considerable cause of our divisions hath been the broaching scandalous names, and employing them to blast the reputation of worthy men; bespattering and aspersing them with insinuations, &c.;—engines devised by spiteful, and applied by simple people;—latitudinarians, rationalists, and I know not what other names, intended for reproach, although importing better signification than those dull detractors can, it seems, discern."—*From an unpublished and unfinished Treatise, "relating to the Dissenters", by Dr. Isaac Barrow.*

relief, they will have so much less inducement to become members of the Establishment; yet if the Establishment make no efforts to unite them to itself, how can this relief be refused them? But if the Establishment were to set its doors widely open, do we doubt that within fifty years the great mass of the dissenting population would gladly enter them? Supposing that habit made the majority of the existing generation of dissenting ministers prefer their own chapels and their own separate society; yet how many of the rising generations, who will now be Dissenters, would eagerly enlist as ministers of the Establishment, if an opening were made for their services by our employing ministers of different stations in society, and exacting from them a less rigid conformity?

I would have no renewal of the Savoy or Hampton Court Conferences; some of the leading Dissenters might be privately consulted, but the alterations to be made in the Liturgy and Articles should be marked out by a Commission,[a] appointed by the king in the first instance, and then submitted to Parliament; and the alterations in the ad-

[a] And above all, I must repeat what I have said before, that this Commission should not consist solely, nor even principally, of Clergymen. The failure of the Commission in 1689 is a warning on this point, as well as against the notion of submitting any plan of Church Reform to the judgment of a Convocation. Previously to this unsuccessful attempt, it had been moved in the House of Lords, "that a number of persons, both of the clergy and laity, should be empowered to prepare such a reformation of things relating to the Church as might be offered to King and Parliament, in order to the healing our divisions," (I am quoting Burnet's words,) "and the correcting what might be amiss or defective in our constitution." Burnet, giving the clergy credit for a sincere desire to promote such a design, wished to leave the matter wholly in their hands, and therefore warmly opposed the motion, which was accordingly rejected. "But I was convinced soon after," he says, "that I had taken wrong measures, and that the method proposed was the only one like to prove effectual."—*History of His Own Times,* Vol. III, p. 11, 8vo edit., London, 1818. Unless we profit, as Burnet did, by his experience, we are likely to meet with a repetition of the same disappointment now.

ministration of the Church should be decided by an act of the legislature, drawn up under the direction of the Government. That the improvements thus effected would at once reconcile many of the Dissenters, and convert many merely nominal Churchmen into hearty friends of the Establishment, appears to me little less than certain. That within fifty years they would nearly extinguish all dissent throughout the kingdom, or reduce it so greatly as to destroy its importance as a national evil, I hold to be in the highest degree probable.

"The proposed comprehension is unchristian." Surely not, as far as the mass of the Protestant Dissenters are concerned, or how could three attempts have been made, in the course of the seventeenth century, to effect it? It matters not whether the ruling party was sincere in its professions; the mere fact of the Hampton Court and Savoy Conferences, to say nothing of the abortive Commission of 1689, is an admission on the part of the Church that a comprehension with those who are called the orthodox Dissenters, cannot be in itself unlawful. I would go farther, and include all who will agree in τὰ ἀναγκαιότατα,—in those points, a denial of which absolutely excludes a man from the Church of Christ. And I hold with Bacon, that the bonds of Christian communion are laid down to be, "One faith,[a] one baptism," not "one ceremonial, one opinion." And further, I think that what Bacon found wanting in his time is wanting still; namely, "a declaration of

[a] "Vincula enim communionis Christianæ ponuntur, *Una fides, unum baptisma,* &c. non unus ritus, una opinio."—"His itaque perpensis, magni videatur res et momenti et usûs esse, et definiatur, qualia sint illa et quantæ latitudinis, quæ ab ecclesiæ corpore homines penitus divellant, et a communione fidelium eliminent. Quod si quis putet, hoc jam pridem factum esse, videat ille etiam atque etiam, quam sincerè et moderatè. Illud interim verisimile est, eum qui pacis mentionem fecerit, reportaturum responsum illud Jehu ad nuntium, '*Numquid pax est, Jehu? Quid tibi et paci? Transi et sequere me.*' Cum non pax sed partes plerisque cordi sint."—*Bacon, De Augmentis Scientiarum,* IX, 1, § 2.

the nature and magnitude of those points which utterly divide men from the Church, and expel them from the communion of the faithful." "And if any man think that this has been done long since," either in the decrees of the four first councils, or in any creeds or articles of any existing Church, "let him observe again and again," as Bacon most justly adds, "how much truth and how much moderation have been shewn in the doing of it." For instance, a false criterion of "fundamental errors" has been set up, in measuring the importance of the error to us by the excellence of the object to which it relates. This has caused men to lay so much stress on all opinions that relate to God. And, indeed, opinions of his moral attributes are of the last importance, because such as we suppose him to be morally, such we strive to become ourselves; but opinions as to his nature metaphysically may be wholly unimportant, because they are often of such a kind as to be wholly inoperative upon our spiritual state: they neither advance us in goodness, nor obstruct our progress in it.

On the other hand, that is *to us* a fundamental error which directly interferes with our own edification. That is to say, we cannot worship with a man who insists upon our omitting some religious exercise which we feel to be important to our own improvement. I laid the stress therefore on the *worship* of Christ, not on the admission of his proper divinity. If a man will not let me pray to and praise my Saviour, he destroys the exercise of my faith altogether; —but I am no way injured by his praying to him as a glorified man, while I pray to him as God. The conclusion to be drawn from the known fallibility of human judgments, is, not that we should be sceptical ourselves, or compromise our own practice, but that we should bear with our neighbour's thinking as he judges right, so long as he will bear with our acting as we judge right. Conformity to our Liturgy therefore is a much better test to require than subscription to our Articles. In other words, if the public prayers of a Church be enough to satisfy a Christian's devotion, and to be an effectual means of grace to him, and if the sacraments be duly administered, we have every thing that is essential to our own improvement; and what has been imagined to afford a greater security to our faith, has, in fact, rather tended to weaken and perplex it.

Of course I am aware that Articles are regarded as a security against erroneous preaching. Now, certainly it would belong to the common discipline of the Church that a minister should not preach against the Liturgy,—he should not contradict the prayers in which he had just before joined. And gross ignorance, and violence, or any indecency of language or manner, might and ought to be noticed by the Church authorities, whose superintendence, if the Church were reformed, would be much more complete and efficient, we might hope, than it is at present. But as to differences of opinion, they exist actually, in spite of the Articles, and all the inconveniences which would arise on that score may be thoroughly appreciated already. We have at this moment the extremes of Calvinism and Arminianism united within the pale of the Establishment;—it is difficult to conceive how any greater differences of opinion could exist, so long as the Liturgy was a Christian Liturgy, and no man was allowed to preach against it.

On Church Government

With respect to Church government, the principal points which I urged were, first, the admission of the laity to a larger share in it;—secondly, that its constitution should be rendered more popular; and, thirdly, that the power of the bishops should be rendered more efficient by the institution of such checks as might allow of its exercise without danger.

I am not aware that on these points Mr. Dickinson's views would differ from mine. He speaks of "the bishop of the diocese, *aided by his proper council*", as if he had no idea that such a limitation of a bishop's power were either unlawful or inexpedient. He is probably not ignorant that in the primitive Church[a] "the bishop did nothing of importance without the advice of his presbyters and deacons," and that "frequently he took the opinion of the whole people." He remembers, that one of the circumstances in the administration of bishops in England, with which Bacon never could be satisfied, was, "the sole exercise of their authority"; that "the bishop giveth orders alone, excommunicateth alone, judgeth alone";—"a thing," he adds, "almost without example in good government."[b] Nor is Mr. Dickinson, so far as appears, one of those extraordinary persons who gravely maintain that primitive Episcopacy, and Episcopacy as it now exists in England, are essentially the same. I was well aware that many persons did maintain this, and I spoke purposely in my pamphlet of the great difference between the two institutions, in order to draw their attention to the grounds on which their belief rested. But as it seems that they are not apt to think out the question for themselves, they are requested to consider the following points.

An office may be said to be essentially the same so long as it is calculated to fulfil equally well the object for which it was originally instituted. Thus, if the object be to perpetuate the dignity and authority of one particular family

[a] "En chaque église l'Evêque ne faisoit rien d'important, sans le conseil des prêtres, des diacres, et des principaux de son clergé. Souvent même il consultoit tout le peuple quand il avoit interêt à l'affaire, comme aux ordinations."—*Fleury, Discours sur l'Histoire des Six Premiers Siècles de l'Eglise,* prefixed to the eighth volume of his *Ecclesiastical History.* This and the other discourses of the same writer, scattered through the volumes of his history, can hardly be recommended too strongly. I know of nothing that at all approaches to them in excellence on the subjects to which they relate. Sir J. Mackintosh has done justice to their merit, in a note in the first volume of his *History of England,* p. 146 (13).

[b] "Of the Pacification of the Church."—*Bacon's Works,* Vol. IV, p. 436. Folio edit. 1730.

or race, the office may be called the same, so long as it is hereditary in this family or race, even though its powers in the course of years may undergo considerable alteration. Thus in an hereditary priesthood, as long as the blood was preserved pure, the office would retain its most essential character of identity, although at one period the priests' power were independent of the civil magistrate, and at another completely subservient to him.

Again, if the object were to secure the continued efficiency of some highly valuable gift, which the possessor for the time being could communicate to any one whom he might fix upon, then the office would be substantially the same so long as the possession of this gift remained annexed to it, although in other matters its powers might be increased or diminished.

But, if the object be simply to provide for the general ends of good government, then the office loses its essential identity so soon as it is altered in those points which affect its operation upon the commonwealth. For instance, the powers of the office may remain the same, but its operation for good or for evil may be wholly different according to the different hands in whom the appointment is vested. No man would call the House of Commons essentially the same, if its members were to be nominated by the crown instead of elected by the people. And, on the other hand, the mode of appointment may remain unchanged, but the character of the office may be essentially changed, by extending its powers or abridging them. The tribunes were still chosen by the tribes as formerly, but the people felt that it was no longer the same office when Sylla deprived it of the right of originating any measure, and made it a disqualification for attaining to all the higher honours in the commonwealth.

Now Episcopacy was clearly not instituted for the sake of maintaining the ascendency of any one family or race; and therefore it has never been hereditary. It is the second case which has given rise to the prevailing confusion on the subject. For the Apostles were possessed of certain most valuable gifts, and could communicate them to others;—and had these gifts been capable of perpetual transmission, the office with which they were transmitted would have remained essentially the same, however much its ordinary powers might have been changed from what they were originally. Now if any gift be thus transmitted in the case of Episcopacy, what is it, and where is the proof of its existence? When men say that the power of ordaining ministers is thus transmitted, there is a confusion in the use of the word *power*. Bishops confer a legal qualification for the ministry, not a real one, whether natural or supernatural. They can give neither piety, nor wisdom, nor learning, nor eloquence;—nothing, in short, but what the laws or constitutions of the Church empower them to give,—that is to say, a commission to preach and to administer the sacraments in the Church of God, according to the measure of the gifts which the person ordained has received, or may receive hereafter, not from them, or through their medium, but from God, and the blessing of the Holy Spirit on his own prayers and exertions.

Episcopacy then was instituted for the general ends of good government; and like ordinary civil offices, its identity depends on its continuing to exercise an equal influence on the welfare of the body connected with it. If then its mode of appointment be wholly changed, and its relation to the Church greatly circumscribed; still more, if the whole society to which it belongs has assumed a different aspect, it is hard to conceive how it can be said to continue essentially the same. Now the primitive bishops were appointed by the members of their own order, with the approbation of the people of the diocese: —bishops in England are appointed solely by the crown. The primitive bishops could legislate for the Church, laity as well as clergy: —the bishops in England can legislate for no one without the consent of the crown,—and if they are allowed to meet in synod, they can legislate only for the clergy,—over the laity their canons have no authority whatever.[a] The primitive bishops fixed the doctrine of their churches, and ordered their ceremonies: —no single bishop, nor all the bishops in England united, can order a single prayer to be added to or taken from the Church service, nor can they so much as alter a single expression in its language. No bishop can ordain any man unless he will take certain oaths imposed by act of parliament, and subscribe to the articles of religion as required by act of parliament. No bishop can refuse to institute any man regularly ordained to any cure of souls in his diocese, to which he may be appointed by the patrons; nor can he, except as patron, and not as bishop, confer the cure of souls on any one. Finally, in the primitive times the bishops were judges in civil matters amongst their people, and thus possessed a temporal influence and authority as well as a spiritual: —whereas in England they are accounted solely the governors of the clergy, and the bulk of the people are hardly aware of their possessing any authority at all.

It will not be supposed that I am dwelling on these differences for the purpose of depreciating our present Episcopacy. Whatever be the faults of our system, it is no reproach to it that it differs from that of the primitive Church. With every thing changed around us, it would be most extraordinary if the same forms of government could continue to suit our altered condition: and to imagine that any one form was intended by the Apostles to be binding upon all Christians, in all times and in all countries, seems to me to betray equal ignorance of the spirit of Christianity, and of the nature and ends of government.

But the change which has taken place in the relations of the Church with the civil power since the first beginning

[a] See Blackstone's Commentaries, Vol. I, p. 83. Edit. Coleridge, 1825.

of Christianity, has been a fruitful subject of dispute. The pretensions of the popes, and of the Roman Catholic clergy in general,—the fanaticism of the Puritans,—and, in later times, some practical inconveniences in our actual system in England, have all helped to embarrass the question.

Church and State

I have charged others with using the word "Church" in a vague or improper sense; and Mr. Dickinson brings the same charge against me. He complains that I have identified the Church in this country with the nation. I plead guilty to the charge, for I do believe them to be properly identical.

The Church, using the word now as synonymous with "Christian society", was instituted for the promotion of man's highest possible perfection and happiness. It did not neglect even his physical wants and sufferings,—but its main object was to improve him morally and spiritually;—to bring him to such a state of goodness and wisdom that his highest happiness would be no longer an unattainable dream.

Now this is precisely the object of civil society also: that is, of the State. Our physical wants may have[a] led to its actual origin, but its proper object is of a higher nature;—it is the intellectual and moral improvement of mankind, in order to their reaching their greatest perfection, and enjoying their highest happiness. This is the object of civil society, or "the State" in the abstract; and the object of any particular civil society or state is still the same, but limited to certain local boundaries which mark the particular subdivisions of the society of mankind.

Civil society aims at the highest happiness of man according to the measure of its knowledge. Religious society aims

[a] *Πόλις—γινομένη μὲν τοῦ ζῆν ἕνεκεν, οὖσα δὲ τοῦ εὖ ζῆν.*—Aristotle, *Politics,* 1, 2.

at it truly and really, because it has obtained a complete knowledge of it. Impart then to civil society the knowledge of religious society, and the objects of both will be not only in intention but in fact the same. In other words, religious society is only civil society fully enlightened: the State in its highest perfection becomes the Church.

When then the individuals of any nation have been converted to Christianity, they see that they had in many instances entertained false and imperfect notions of their highest perfection and happiness. Their mistakes are now corrected; what they thought was the summit of the mountain, they now find to be a point of inferior height: but their object is still the same as it was before,—to reach the top of the mountain. Institutions may be modified, laws amended, wars may become less frequent and less bloody, the practice of the nation may be substantially changed, but still it is pursuing the same object as before; only with the advantage of discerning it more clearly, and following it more steadily.

But the case has been perplexed, by its being supposed that civil and religious society have necessarily two distinct governments; that the magistrate is at the head of the one, and the priest of the other; and that these two offices have a different tenure; the one deriving its authority from human law, from custom, from mutual agreement, or from superior force, while the other was derived from the express command of God, and handed down in an unbroken succession from those whom God first invested with it.

Of two powers with such pretensions neither could be expected to yield to the other. And the alleged distinctness of their titles hindered them from coalescing; the State not choosing to take its rulers from those who boasted to possess already a higher title to authority than the State could give them, while the Church regarded it as a profanation to place rulers made by man on a level with those appointed by God. Offices so distinct naturally kept up the belief that the societies to which they respectively belonged were essentially distinct also.

But the error consisted in ascribing to Christianity an office which it does not recognize on earth,—that of the priesthood. Grant that there is a priesthood, that is, an order of men deriving their authority from God only, through the medium of one another, and you introduce at once into the relations of civil and religious society an element of perpetual disunion. It will for ever be a question whether the State is to rule the Church, or the Church the State, or if they are supposed to meet as allies with one another, yet one or the other party will be for ever complaining that the terms of the alliance are not strictly kept to.

The New Testament, amongst a thousand other proofs of that divine wisdom in which Christianity originated, offers this most remarkable one,—that alone of all the religions of civilized man it disclaims any earthly priesthood. The Christian society had its ministers of various ranks and various offices; but nothing was definitely and universally commanded with regard to their numbers, jurisdiction, or mode of appointment. As far as related to its external constitution, it was left from age to age in full possession of the right of regulating its own government.

Now, whilst the civil society was distinct from the religious one, it is manifest that the civil offices belonging to the latter must have held a very subordinate place, because those of the highest dignity and importance were exclusively in the hands of the former. The highest earthly ministers of God's moral government, that is to say, those persons who were invested with the supreme executive and legislative power, could not be ministers of His spiritual government also, because they were not yet acquainted with it. Yet as their jurisdiction, and the benefits of their functions, extended to the members of the religious society, the exercise of similar functions by these last was at once unnecessary and impossible. The great work of civil society was already done for them by others; not perfectly indeed, because it proceeded from men who had not the benefit of their wisdom, but yet so as to preclude them from attempting to do it for themselves.

But no sooner had civil society become enlightened, and learned aright what was the destiny of man, what his greatest perfection, and what his highest happiness, than it became at once a religious society, but armed with powers, and grown to a fulness of stature, which religious society till now had never known. The civil offices which it now had to discharge were no longer subordinate and municipal, but sovereign and national; nor did they lose their inherent supremacy, because they were administered on higher principles. The King had been the head of the State, he was equally the head of the perfected State, that is, of the Church; with him rested the duty of disposing and superintending all the details of the society's government, so as to make them most effective towards the attainment of its great object, the highest perfection and happiness of the community. And the "King", in this statement, is merely another name for the supreme power in society; so that what is true of the individual sovereign in a pure monarchy, is true equally of the bodies of men, be they more or less numerous, by whom the sovereignty is exercised in an aristocracy or a democracy.

When this sovereign power then directs and controls its inferior ministers, the clergy, and legislates for the great objects of the society, by providing for the highest instruction of its members, and taking care that it be at once pure and effective; it is not that the State is governing the Church, but that the Church, through the medium of its supreme government, is ruling itself. The confusion has arisen from the notion, that the highest ministers of the Church must *always* be bishops or presbyters, because they were so in the days of its existence as a subordinate and municipal society. Even had the Christian ministers of religion been a priesthood, yet the example of the Israelites might teach us that Moses is greater than Aaron,—that he who rules God's people to direct them in the ways of judgment, mercy, and truth, is greater than he who ministers at the altar. Much more are Christian rulers greater than the Christian clergy, inasmuch as the functions of the latter, not being definitely fixed by any divine law, are far more subject to the control of the supreme government of the Church than were the offices of the Jewish priesthood.

What I have here stated are the true principles of the Church of England, upon which she asserted, in opposition to the Roman Catholics and to the Presbyterians,—that the King is the supreme head of the Church on earth. "It was certainly designed at one time," says Mr. Dickinson, "that the Church and the nation should be co-extensive." I should rather say that the founders of the Protestant Church of England considered them as identical:—the Christian nation of England was the Church of England;—the head of that nation was for that very reason the head of the Church;—the public officers of the nation, whether civil or ecclesiastical, were officers therefore of the Church;—and every Englishman was supposed to be properly a member of it,—baptized into it almost as soon as he was born,—taught its lessons in his early childhood,—required to partake of its most solemn pledge of communion[a],—married under its sanction and blessing,—and laid in the grave within its peculiar precincts, amidst its prayers and most affectionate consolations. And is it indifference or latitudinarianism to

[a] "And note that every parishioner shall communicate at the least three times in the year."—*Rubrick at the end of the Communion Service.*—See also the Prayer for the Church militant, and the second Collect for Good Friday, as beautiful instances of the extensive sense in which our reformers used the word "Church". In the former, the King's Council, the Judges, &c., are prayed for as officers in the Church, before even the Bishops and Curates.—See also Romans xii. 6-8.

wish most devoutly that this noble, this divine theory, may be fully and for ever realized?[b]

It is owing to the existence of religious dissent that not only is it not realized in practice, but its very truth and excellence are disputed. And that dissent has arisen out of faults and errors on both sides, on the part of the Dissenters no less than on that of the Church, is a fact which no impartial man can doubt. It may be too late now to remedy the mischief entirely; but surely if it be remedied even in part it will be no light benefit,—and it is absurd to suppose that it can be remedied at all without an alteration, or rather an enlargement, of our present ecclesiastical consti-

[b] It is objected to this doctrine, that it implies the exclusion of those who are not members of the Church from the civil rights of citizens. I think it does imply such an exclusion in the case of those who are not members of the Church of Christ: nor should I consider a Christian nation justified in forming a legislative union with a nation of Jews, or Mahometans, or Heathens. If the citizens of the same nation are in nearly equal proportion Christians and Heathens, the State in that country is not yet sufficiently enlightened to become a Church;—and it is here that our Lord's words apply, that "his kingdom is not of this world":—Christians have no right, as such, to press the establishment of their religion to the prejudice of the civil rights of others. Yet if the two religions happened to be for the most part locally divided, it would be a reason why such a nation should separate itself into two, and the Christian and Heathen portions of it form each a state distinct from the other. But when the decided majority of a country become Christians, so that the State may justly become a Church, then the Heathen part of the population ought to be excluded from the legislature, and encouraged, if it be possible, to emigrate to other countries, if they complain of not participating in the full rights of citizenship. At present, in England, I should earnestly deprecate the admission of the Jews to a share in the national legislature. It is a principle little warranted by authority or by reason, that the sole qualification for enjoying the rights of citizenship should consist in being locally an inhabitant of any country. But all professing Christians, of whatever sect, as being members of the Church of Christ, must be supposed to have much more in common with each other, as far as the great ends of society are concerned, than they have points of difference. Their peculiar tenets, therefore, need form no ground for their exclusion.

tution and ritual. Therefore I earnestly desire such an enlargement, and I look to the supreme government of the Church,—the government of this still Christian nation,—as the only power by which it can or ought to be effected. Let it be supposed chimerical to expect any extensive comprehension of the Dissenters; even then the relaxing of the uniformity of the Liturgy, the reduction of the size of the dioceses, and the increase of their number, the appointment of additional orders of ministers, which might include members of the poorer classes, and, above all, the conferring on the lay members of the Church a greater share in its ordinary administration, would be productive of the greatest benefit, inasmuch as it would interest many in the welfare of the Church, who now, without being Dissenters, feel that they have little to do with it, and habitually look upon it as the concern of the clergy, and not their own. Such a reform, too, might make the Church effective, where its exertions are most needed, and where they are at present necessarily most inefficient; I mean, amongst the masses of our manufacturing population. Indeed, when we consider the utter inadequacy of the Establishment, as it now stands, to meet the wants of the great manufacturing towns and districts, it may be said that in those portions of the kingdom our business is not so much to reform the Church, as to create one.

Undoubtedly if that large part of our population, who are at present neither Churchmen nor Dissenters, could be really attached to the Established Church, the danger arising from the existence of avowed dissent would be greatly lessened. We might then hope to save the Establishment; which must always be a great blessing, however much its usefulness and excellence may be impaired by exclusiveness. But as things now are, in any attempts to attach the people to the Church, we find that the Dissenters actually oppose us; and this, it is to be feared, will always be the case, unless a more comprehensive system be adopted. If this fear be ill-founded; if the Church, without any alteration of its Articles, or Liturgy, or government, can succeed in working its way amidst the manufacturing population; can improve them physically and morally, and make them sensible of the benefits which they receive from it; there is not a man alive to whom this proof of its inherent vitality will be more grateful than to me. Were it even more exclusive than it is, its preservation would still be earnestly to be desired, as one of the greatest national blessings. Most heartily do I wish to see it reformed, at once for the sake of its safety and of its greater perfection; but, reformed or not, may God, in His mercy, save us from the calamity of seeing it destroyed.

NOTES

on the text of

Principles of Church Reform

1. This and succeeding paragraphs owe much to S. T. Coleridge's *Constitution of Church and State,* 1830.

2. This state of affairs obtained in France from the Concordat in 1801 between Napoleon I and the Papacy, until the Separation of Church and State in 1905.

3. Lucius Cary, 2nd Viscount Falkland, 1610-1643; published a *Discourse on Infallibility* and two discourses on *Episcopacy.*

4. Joseph Priestley, 1733-1804, the distinguished Unitarian theologian and scientist, who held various pastoral charges, was a tutor at Warrington Academy, 1761-1767, and tutor to Lord Shelborne's sons, 1773-1780. After the Birmingham riots he moved to Hackney, was made a citizen of France in 1792, and went to America in 1794.

5. Cf. Introduction, p. 61.

6. A general account of the reforms achieved in the decades after Arnold's pamphlet is to be found in E. L. Woodward, *The Age of Reform* 1815-1870, Oxford, Clarendon Press, 1954, 1st ed. 1938, pp. 483-509.

7. *Miscellaneous Sonnets.*

8. Since Arnold wrote the Americans have proved competent analysts of their religion. The contemporary developments of that religious pluralism upon which Arnold comments are the subject of a notable study by Will Herberg, *Protestant-Catholic-Jew,* New York, Doubleday, 1956, which draws upon a wealth of sociological and theological writing.

9. William Winstanley Hull, 1794-1873, with whom Arnold frequently corresponded—a lawyer with an interest in liturgical reform. The quotation is from his *Thoughts on Church Reform,* 1832.

10. Gilbert Burnet, 1643-1715; involved in the struggle for power between episcopalians and presbyterians in the Scottish Church in Charles II's reign; one of the chief agents of William and Mary's "Glorious Revolution"; Bishop of Salisbury, 1689, a conscientious diocesan bishop while a great figure in the nation. He stood for toleration and comprehension; was a member of the Comprehension

Commission, 1689. One of his achievements was the creation of Queen Anne's Bounty for the augmentation of livings.

11. The author was the German Roman Catholic biblical critic, Johann Leonhard Hug, 1765-1846.

12. Cf. "Observations of Ecclesiastical Legislature and Church Reform" (1833), in *Remains of the Most Reverend Charles Dickinson, D.D., Lord Bishop of Meath, being a selection from his Sermons and Tracts*; biographical sketch by the Reverend J. West, London, B. Fellowes, 1845, pp. 267-342, esp. pp. 305-33.

Charles Dickinson; born 1792; domestic chaplain and secretary to the Archbishop of Dublin (Richard Whately, cf. Introduction, n. 59), 1833; consecrated Bishop of Meath, December 1840; like Arnold died prematurely in July, 1842, a few weeks after Arnold's death.

One of Dickinson's wittiest and most penetrating publications was the "Pastoral Epistle from His Holiness the Pope to some Members of the University of Oxford", *Remains,* pp. 221-66, written after the first two of the five volumes of *Tracts for the Times* had appeared and underlining their Romanizing tendency.

He shared Arnold's and Whately's concern for Church reform as other writings in the *Remains* show. His main point of difference with Arnold, whose views he treats with respect, was Arnold's identification of Church and State.

13. Sir James Mackintosh, 1765-1832; published a notable reply to Burke's attack on the French Revolution, 1791; Recorder of Bombay, 1803; Member of Parliament, 1813; Professor of Law at Haileybury, 1818-1824. His chief works were *Dissertation of the Progress of Ethical Philosophy,* 1830, and *History of the Revolution in England in 1688,* 1834. Charles Darwin called him "the best converser I ever listened to". *The Autobiography of Charles Darwin, 1809-1882,* ed. Nora Barlow, Collins, 1958, p. 55.

BIBLIOGRAPHY

1. Thomas Arnold's Works

Six volumes of *Sermons* (1829, 1832, 1832-4, 1835-41, 1841-2, one volume mainly on the Interpretation of Scripture).

Two Sermons on Prophecy, 1839.

Fragments on Church and State, posthumous.

Editions of *Thucydides,* 3 vols., 1830, 1833, 1835.

History of Rome, 3 vols., 1838, 1840, 1842.

History of the later Roman Commonwealth, 2 vols.

Introductory Lectures on Modern History, 1842.

The Miscellaneous Works of Thomas Arnold, 1845, edited by A. P. Stanley, including:

The Christian Duty of Conceding the Roman Catholic Claims, 1828.
The Englishman's Register, articles signed A., 1831.
Letters to the Sheffield Courant, 1831-2.
Principles of Church Reform, with postscript, 1833.
The Order of Deacons, 1841.
Letters to the Hertford Reformer, 1839-41.

Among articles was "Dr. Hampden" (*Edinburgh Review,* Vol. LXIII, 1836).

2. Some pamphlets on Church Reform at the time of *Principles of Church Reform* and replies to Arnold

L. Carpenter, *Brief Notes on the Rev. Dr. Arnold's Principles of Church Reform,* 1833.

C. Dickinson, *Observations on Ecclesiastical Legislative and Church Reform,* 1833.

Lord Robert Henley, *A Plan for Church Reform,* 1832.

Ed. J. Manning, *Church Reform,* extracts from the writings of eminent divines of the Established Church, relative to its further Reformation, 1832.

W. Palmer, *Remarks on the Rev. Dr. Arnold's Principles of Church Reform,* 1833.

J. Yates, *The Grounds of Dissent from the Church of England not materially diminished by the present prospects of ecclesiastical reform,* with an appendix containing remarks on Dr. Arnold's *Principles of Church Reform,* 1833.

3. Books and articles on Thomas Arnold

T. W. Bamford, *Thomas Arnold,* 1960.

R. J. Campbell, *Thomas Arnold,* 1927.

J. J. Findley, *Arnold of Rugby, His School Life and Contribution to Education,* 1897.

C. K. Gloyn, *The Church in the Social Order,* A Study of Anglican Social Theory from Coleridge to Maurice, 1942.

J. Martineau, "The Life and Correspondence of Thomas Arnold" in *Prospective Review,* February 1845.

J. B. Mozley, "Dr. Arnold" (*Christian Remembrances,* October 1844).

J. Middleton Murry, *The Price of Leadership,* 1939.

J. A. W. Neander, *The Theology of Thomas Arnold,* 1846.

D. Payne, "Christianizing the Nation and Edifying the Church" (*Theology,* LIX, 1956).

Extract from the *Record* Newspaper, "Brief Observations on the political and religious sentiments of the late Rev. Dr. Arnold as contained in the 'Life' by the Rev. A. P. Stanley", 1845.

A. P. Stanley, *Life and Correspondence of Dr. Arnold,* 1844 (Teachers' Edition, 1901).

G. L. Strachey, *Eminent Victorians,* 1918.

A. G. Stuart, *Examination of a tract entitled Brief Observations etc.,* 1845.

W. G. Ward, "Review of Arnold's Sermons" (*British Critic,* October 1841).

A. Whitridge, *Dr. Arnold of Rugby*, 1928.

B. Willey, *Nineteenth Century Studies*, 1949.

N. Wymer, *Dr. Arnold of Rugby*, 1953.

Anon., "Review of Arnold's Sermons" (*British Critic*, April 1830).

4. Background Studies

G. F. A. Best, "The Constitutional Revolution, 1828-1832" (*Theology*, LXII, 1959).

O. J. Brose, *Church and Parliaments, The Reshaping of the Church of England, 1828-1860*, 1959.

S. C. Carpenter, *Church and People, 1689-1889*, 1933.

S. T. Coleridge, *On the Constitution of Church and State*, 1829.

C. Dickinson, *Remains of the Most Reverend Charles Dickinson, D.D. Lord Bishop Meath, Being a Selection from his Sermons and Tracts*, 1845.

E. Halévy, *A History of the English People in the Nineteenth Century*, 1951.

J. L. and Barbara Hammond, *The Bleak Age*, 1934. *The Age of the Chartists, 1832-1854*, 1930.

W. L. Mathieson, *English Church Reform, 1815-1840*, 1923.

Ed. H. Reeve, *The Grenville Memoirs*: a Journal of the Reigns of King George IV and King William IV, by the late Charles C. F. Greville, 2nd ed., 1874.

L. Trilling, *Matthew Arnold*, 1939.

E. L. Woodward, *The Age of Reform, 1815-1870*, 1938.